Children and Art Teaching

CROOM HELM TEACHING 5-13 SERIES
Edited by Colin Richards, formerly of the School of Education,
Leicester University.

Assessment in Primary and Middle Schools
Marten Shipman

Organising Learning in the Primary School Classroom
Joan Dean

Development, Experience and Curriculum in Primary Education
W.A.L. Blyth

Place and Time with Children Five to Nine
Joan Blyth

Children and Art Teaching

KEITH GENTLE

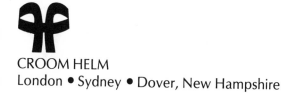

CROOM HELM
London • Sydney • Dover, New Hampshire

© 1985 K. Gentle
Croom Helm Ltd, Provident House, Burrell Row,
Beckenham, Kent BR3 1AT
Croom Helm Australia Pty Ltd, First Floor,
139 King Street, Sydney, NSW 2001, Australia

British Library Cataloguing in Publication Data

Gentle, Keith
    Children and art teaching. — (Croom Helm
    teaching 5-13 series)
    1. Arts — Study and teaching (Elementary)
    — Great Britain
    I. Title
    372.5'044'0941   N4343
    ISBN 0-7099-1122-X
    ISBN 0-7099-1123-8 Pbk

Croom Helm, 51 Washington St.,
Dover, New Hampshire 03820, USA

Library of Congress Cataloging in Publication Data

Gentle, Keith, 1934-
    Children and art teaching.

    (Croom Helm teaching 5-13 series)
    1. Art — Study and teaching (Elementary) — United
States.   2. Learning by discovery.   I. Title
II. Series
N362.G46   1984   372.5'044   84-17615
    ISBN 0-7099-1122-X
    ISBN 0-7099-1123-8 Pbk

Typeset by Leaper & Gard, Bristol, England

Printed and bound in Great Britain by
Biddles Ltd, Guildford and King s Lynn

CONTENTS

FIGURES

ACKNOWLEDGEMENTS

The contract to write this book was signed at a most difficult time, when I was due to be made redundant or re-deployed by my Education Authority. It was, if you like, an act of faith that despite everything I decided to make the attempt.

Tricia Steel has been a constant source of support and encouragement in this venture, in discussing, reading and re-reading the script.

I am grateful to Roy Whitehouse and Charlie Naylor for giving time to read the early drafts and for making thoughtful and perceptive comments. I am grateful, also, to Robin Tanner for allowing me to use part of one of his talks.

Julia McKiddie forged her way through my writing to get the script typed.

Lastly, I am grateful to Colin Richards for his professional and helpful comments and to the publishers for their patience.

To two generations
  my Mother
    and my children
RICHARD, MICHAEL & DIANA

FOREWORD

Teaching 5-13 is a series of books intended to foster the professional development of teachers in primary and middle schools. The series is being published at a time when there are growing demands on teachers to demonstrate increasing levels of professional understanding and competence. Although the importance of personal qualities and social skills in successful teaching is acknowledged, the series is based on the premisses that the enhancement of teacher competence and judgement in curricular and organisational matters is the major goals of pre-service and in-service teacher education and that this enhancement is furthered, not by the provision of recipes to be applied in any context, but by the application of practical principles for the organisation and management of learning, and for the planning, implementation and evaluation of curricula. The series aims to help teachers and trainee teachers to think out for themselves ways of tackling the problems which confront them in their own particular range of circumstances. It does this by providing two kinds of books: those which focus on a particuar area of the primary or middle school curriculum and those which discuss general issues germane to any area of the curriculum.

In this book Keith Gentle explores the teaching of art — an area of the primary curriculum about which too little has been written in recent years (except for books dealing with techniques and those offering ideas for instant 'art-making'). In doing so, he provides an original introduction to children's development in general and to their visual, spatial and tactile development in particular. Curriculum design, assessment and evaluation, and the choice of materials are also considered along with a dynamic model of art teaching. The book provides a much needed introduction to the complexities, challenges and tensions involved in fostering children's development in art in an authentic, sensitive yet disciplined way.

Colin Richards

INTRODUCTION

Teaching 5-13

It is a truism to say that the job of teaching is to teach. This assumption has been persistently questioned in the field of art education and has perhaps been one of the central dilemmas in primary education over the last thirty years.

To teach or not; to intervene, to direct, to instruct, to demonstrate or not. This dilemma is to be found no more acutely than in art education where there are perennial arguments about such topics as whether to demonstrate or not; whether to teach technique; whether to use the blackboard or work on a child's picture.

Whatever techniques or gimmicks are culled from books, television or magazines, the problem of how to teach them will not go away. How are results achieved if not through teaching and instruction? Do children produce exciting work in art if the teacher does not interfere but merely provides the materials and stimuli?

It could be argued that the development of teaching skills is very much to do with the way each person finds his or her route through this dilemma. It is not as simple as an either teach or don't-teach situation. In a number of important ways, this book hopes to clarify this dilemma and propose solutions.

At one time teachers would be inspired by a sense of vocation to surmount such considerations as how to teach. Many have felt a professional pride and dedication in what they do. There was also a feeling of security within the profession which gave confidence to each one to find their own way, to ask questions, and to work out solutions appropriate to their own situation and particular group of children. Of course this produced a mixture of approaches and had a varied range of success. The idiosyncracy of British education was, and still is, demonstrated in personal and eclectic approaches.

However, philosophy apart, I doubt whether anyone can teach with confidence unless they have certain ideas or beliefs which give their practice some personal direction and meaning. If this is so, then from where do such personal meanings and directions come?

They certainly seem to arise from the climate of practice which every teacher meets when they become a member of a school staff. An individual can be influenced in all kinds of ways: by the way in which children's work is or is not displayed, by the choice of topics and materials to carry them out, by the kinds of things other teachers do and by the expectations they feel that the head teacher and colleagues have of them. All these and many more subtle and pervasive details of the school day, easily overlooked by the visitor, affect the ideas and values of the teacher and the way he or she works with children.

The school climate will also be subject continually to subtle shifts in emphasis. The most obvious and marked time for these to occur is on the appointment of a new headteacher or when a school changes its designation. The climate will also be affected by expressions of view in the press, government surveys, DES reports, the approaches of local and national inspectorate. The attitude of parents and public is also increasingly affecting the climate in which teaching takes place and personal satisfaction and meaning can be discovered by the teacher.

In all these matters it is important to sort out those things over which an individual can have some control, and those which are out of range or too diffuse to be changed directly. Thus, the organisation of the teaching area, the way that preparation and readiness to work are achieved, the relationship to children and how they learn to use and contribute to the classroom environment, are all things over which the teacher has control. The attitudes of those outside school, the policies and pronouncements of public bodies, are not.

This book is about teaching children from five to thirteen in the field of art. This age span represents a wide and profoundly important period of time in the growth of children as every teacher and parent knows. Therefore it would be foolish to discuss teaching without considering the kinds of changes which characterise the different phases of development in children. In terms of the present book these have, as far as possible, been related to the child's visual, spatial and tactile development and are based on personal observations and the studies of teachers and art educators. It is hoped that those reading this book will consider their own observations and insights into children alongside those offered here.

Apart from these thoughts it is also important to consider visual matters in their own right as being significant ways of understanding the world around us. A number of underlying ideas are used when considering the working environment, the most suitable materials to use and ways of stimulating an awareness in children of the way things look and feel, grow or are constructed, and how materials behave. Similarly, approaches to looking at children's art and the work of artists, craftsmen and designers are considered.

Example aims are suggested in order to share some of the possible ways of planning a curriculum and building a syllabus and reasons are given for doing so. It is hoped that the approaches described in the book to these and other matters, such as working with children and assessing and recording their work, will be seen as possible ways of thinking rather than examples to be followed.

The approach of this book aims to bring out the importance for every teacher of making up his or her own mind about what is important, what emphasis to place on it and how it should be approached. The arguments and examples are meant to stimulate, provoke and support such personal endeavour, not supplant it.

It has often been said that the most beneficial experience for teachers is in carrying out research or curriculum development and not in merely applying the findings of someone else. There is much to be said for this attitude and I would hope that this book stimulates and guides others into that kind of activity.

The book starts with a consideration of babyhood as this is a period of high sensitivity to sensations and impressions which form the foundation for later experience. There follows a possible developmental scheme which places, in the perspective of our growth, certain important moments when we change and our potential for certain kinds of development is increased

After these opening chapters the book gets to the main ideas concerning teaching five- to thirteen-year-olds, starting with the first moments at school, and developing through to the threshold of adolescence. Approaches to teaching art are considered along with examples of curriculum thinking and building a syllabus.

There is then a chapter on assessment and evaluation which again uses example aims and uses these as a basis for showing how assessment and evaluation might be thought about and developed. Reasons are given for the need for teachers to make assessments in art and suggestions as to how such activity can actually assist the teacher.

The book could not be complete without some consideration of the most suitable materials to use and why their characteristics make them the right choice for certain kinds of art work.

1 BEGINNINGS

This chapter introduces the two major themes of the book: the need for continual sensory enrichment in the growth of children and the search for personal meaning in the lives of each individual. Sensory nourishment of babies leads to a discussion of exploration and control as two important modes of learning and the relationship of sensitivity to them. Particular kinds of energy are considered especially in regard to firsthand experience and its potential for learning. Lastly, the need to communicate and the different ways in which children do this is seen in relation to the visual means to do so. What we choose to communicate and the means we achieve to do so depends as much on the meanings with which we invest our experience as the way in which we are understood.

It may appear unusual to start a book on teaching five- to thirteen-year-olds by referring to birth. However, in discussing the needs or shortcomings of any particular group of students or pupils it is not unusual for teachers to refer, often disparagingly, to what should have taken place at an earlier period. At all levels, dissatisfaction with the achievements of earlier upbringing and schooling is not uncommon. What is perhaps more unusual is an effort by the critics to attempt to really understand the problems and peculiarities of an earlier period of development.

It is partly for this reason that I unashamedly start by referring to birth and also because I believe that there are a number of characteristic and easily distinguished modes of experience which form the basis of all later developments.

A number of years ago I came across the work of the French obstetrician, Frederick Leboyer,[1] who had decided to rethink his approach to delivering babies after twenty-five years of traditional practice. The traditional approach to birth subjected the delicate senses of the baby, at the moment of birth, to bright lights, a harsh, clinical environment and almost immediate separation from the mother-support by the cutting of the umbilical cord. Leboyer believed that birth should be handled with much greater sensitivity to the existence of the baby and the direct sensory experience

1

which is the beginning of its new life.

Therefore the transition from womb life to outside, detached life is handled differently by Leboyer and those using his methods. In a softly lit room, the child is first laid on the mother's abdomen, and not until the umbilical cord ceases to pulse is it cut, and then the child is laid in a bath of blood-heat water, where it is gently supported, as in the bag of waters.

Whether one believes that such perceptions about the needs of babies have significance in their development will depend as much on one's perceptions of oneself as on established medical or psychological precept. I refer to the ideas of Leboyer in order to focus attention on an aspect of his belief which I wish to develop in relation to children's growth through art. Susannah Kent in an article on Laboyer wrote,

> The baby is stroked and washed following the belief that by returning him to a watery environment similar to that of the womb, he can begin gradually and without shock to explore the sensations of his body and the feelings of separateness which are the beginning of his new life.

Embedded in this passage are the two major themes of this book, which I will endeavour to relate to children's growth and the task of teaching in art. I see the exploration of sensation as being fundamental to the development of young children and, beyond this, as being an essential ingredient to the development of visual, tactile and spatial imagery in older children and adults.

Secondly, I sense that feelings of separateness are the source of personal endeavour to make sense of experience and lead the individual, eventually, to strive after meanings and images that give life coherence.

I will pursue these two ideas in this chapter and refer to them in other sections of the book.

Sensory Exploration

We know that young babies explore their immediate world in a direct, sensory way. Initially they grasp and suck, respond to sounds and the presence of the mother. Gradually, as limbs grow and become stronger, they probe and touch, enjoying and developing sensation or withdrawing from it. We can observe how this establishes patterns of action and reaction in the baby and can infer that physical patterns which can be seen reflect hidden patterns in the mind of which they are evidence. In her book *Children's Minds* Margaret Donaldson quotes experimental work with very young babies which shows clearly that they begin to control what they do as well as explore direct sensation.[2] The inference based on such observation of babies is that patterns of understanding are being laid down in their minds which form a basis of their view of the world. Daniel Stern in his book *First Relationship: Infant and Mother*[3] suggests that this 'view of the world' resides in the oldest part of the human brain and that this part of the brain drives the body towards interactions with its environment. He further suggests that it is the action of these primary perceptions that enables the baby to form bonds with the earth. Such interactions in babies and infants are direct, spontaneous and egocentric (self-centred). Reality is as it is to the child at the moment of perception and centred on the self and its responses.

Although as adults, we grow away from the need to experience directly the sensation of things that are part of our environment, it is apparent that our need for physical, sensory experience is very strong, even though we may not equate it directly with our capacity to learn and earn a living. The enormous amount of time spent in leisure pursuits and relaxation, which take us into direct physical and sensory contact with the environment, is a clear indication of the need for first-hand experience.

Therefore the need to experience freshly and certainly for ourselves remains and is crucial in any instances where we wish to express ourselves through materials of any kind. Therefore exploration of materials and media is fundamental to the development of an individual's powers of expression and communication; it is through such exploration that knowledge of materials and media and their potential for creating expressive and communicative forms is achieved. However, levels of personal control are necessary to attain such forms and arise as an outcome of exploration. A characteristic of the human mind is that it needs to form patterns from experience.

In writing this, I am clearly linking control with exploration because I believe that it is self-evident that where any development or progress takes place there must be personal control as well as personal exploration. However, these two ways of engaging in experience can be contradictory: on the one hand, if we organise and control an activity, we can limit the way in which new discoveries are made and further opportunities created for development; on the other hand, unless we find ways to control and order the activity, any exploration can remain formless and lack personal direction.

The apparent contradiction between exploration and control is found in different forms at all levels of education and creative human endeavour and I will draw on this dichotemy during the development of this book.

In relation to the present discussion, it is important to recognise the nature of such a contradiction; that is, both modes of experience (exploration and control) are essential ways of engaging with the world of materials and objects, yet they have the potential to be exclusive. This is especially so when considered together with the teacher/pupil relationship, which has been interpreted traditionally as the former organising, structuring and controlling the learning of the latter. What an individual learns, how it is assimilated, the time taken and the connections made with other learning are all more mysterious rather than explicit activities to the teacher. What becomes evident is that certain situations and personalities seem to make it easier than others for personal learning to take place and there is always the potential for actual tension or conflict to arise between the teacher's control of learning and the pupil's personal need to explore it in his own way.

It will be evident that this is an oversimplified statement of the relationship in practice, for the 'control' mode is modified by the 'exploratory' one and vice-versa. Perhaps the successful teacher is able to achieve a balance between these two modes of experience and thus ensure that learning progresses both positively and personally. However, the actual situation is not as simple as this suggests, for it is more usual for there to be a continual flux between activities which are characteristically exploratory or controlling, with one initiating the need for the other.

The teacher cannot be saying 'Get on with your work' all the time, and will have to employ other actions if the child is to become involved purposefully in the learning. The interaction between the child's learning and the teacher's teaching will be discussed more fully in Chapter 6. What is important to realise here is that whatever kinds of actions the teacher promotes, the need to achieve a balance between exploration and control is paramount.

Such a balance will be sought between the teacher and the child as well as between the child and his work. If this is so, then what is it which achieves this state of balance? What other mode of experience is present which relates exploration and control in such a way that they are not mutually exclusive but mutually relevant and necessary?

The third mode of experience which achieves this balance I believe to be sensitivity. Sensitivity is defined as 'an awareness and readiness for change'.[4] Obviously change is a key issue in education. In all kinds of ways and at different levels, change is accessible to observation and different kinds of measurement. If it were not so we could never know whether it had taken place. Physical changes which promote such developments as increased co-ordination and finer motor skill are one example. Changes in alertness, attention and the capacity to respond are others.

I understand this definition through visualising the way in which growth takes place, not particularly physical growth, although this is closely related, but growth in perception and the capacity to communicate.

Young babies grow at an enormous rate, attaining, on average, half adult height by the third year. Where any organism is growing at that kind of speed, it is very sensitive to all kinds of influences and sensations. Therefore, it is not just the range of experience in which the child engages but also the sensitive quality of the relationship which promotes the child's growth.

The sensitivity with which the child explores is obviously significant and related closely to the trust and confidence which the child feels. This can also be true of the ways in which a child learns to control his actions and responses, so that they reinforce confidence and open up new horizons for activity.

Thus the patterns which form in the baby's mind as he grows are closely related to the sensitivity with which he is able to explore and control his experience of the world. Furthermore, this notion leads me to a richer understanding of how we learn, whether at the infant stage or later, through the apparent contradiction between exploration and control being resolved by the sensitivity with which they are performed.

In other words, where the exploration is sensitive the control becomes more personal and is related to the appropriate level that can be managed, and where the control is sensitive it gives confidence to the individual and enables him to see further potential in the experience.

In this way sensitivity relates exploration to control in such a way that they are mutually relevant and necessary and certainly not exclusive. They may easily be divorced by the over-insistence by a parent or teacher on the learning taking place in specific ways or having to be demonstrated in narrow and formal ways that are inappropriate to the learner and the task being undertaken.

The following diagram may help to make this more explicit:

Modes of experience

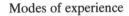

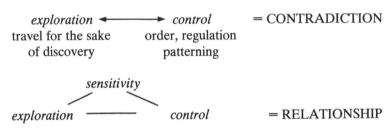

exploration ⟷ *control*		= CONTRADICTION
travel for the sake	order, regulation	
of discovery	patterning	

sensitivity

exploration ——— *control*		= RELATIONSHIP

Later it will be necessary to look at these modes of experience and their relationship in other ways, for example when we consider the role of the teacher and the kind of teaching strategies which each mode promotes. It is worth saying here that an approach which emphasises control is very different from one which emphasises exploration. The provision of time, resources and space would all tend to be different and shift away from a balanced relationship towards polarity, especially when under pressure.

The significant issue, especially in art education, is what kind of approach promotes sensitivity and how does it extend the potential for learning? These issues will be taken up later in this chapter and in subsequent chapters. It is now necessary to consider sensitivity in another way, namely, the quality of energy it employs.

Energy

Apart from considering exploration and control as ways of experiencing there is another way in which we should consider them. It is clear that we all have a certain amount of energy to deploy on the various tasks and demands that confront us each day. There are different kinds of energy — for example, direct, physical energy enabling us to move about and work in our environment, or perceptual energy with which we focus on particular elements in any environment in order to recognise them or see them freshly.

In relation to the exploration/control model I wish to characterise two forms of energy, namely, that which is active and outgoing and that which is receptive and in-flowing.

The first is the energy which flows out from the individual into the task of manipulating the maze of people, places, objects and events which confront him/her during the course of a day. This energy is more akin to scanning and enables the individual to select rapidly and almost immediately those things necessary to take in or avoid so that they achieve their immediate ends. Those familiar things which comfort, distress, assuage desire, satisfy the need to let off energy and so on and fall within the known experience of the individual are managed by this out-going energy.

The second form of energy is the in-flowing, receptive and assimilative kind of energy which absorbs experience and reflects upon it. This arises much more from a particular focusing of the attention, through curiosity, interest or individual will. The sensations arising from this can be concentrated and seem to effect a change in the way that the individual feels and thinks. Such an in-flowing of sensation has the potential to change the way in which the individual behaves and understands the world around him. This form of energy also seems to require a certain stillness and attention.

Both forms of energy are obviously related by the sensitivity with which they are used, so that the outward negotiation with the environment is more alert and aware of the effect of change and response within, and the responses within are able to open up and enrich the way the environment is seen and enjoyed. This kind of reciprocal action is experienced when we go into a new town, where our experience of towns gives us a rough idea of what to expect and our outward-looking helps us to find it. But the enjoyment or otherwise of the sensations (visual, spatial, auditory and so on) of being there can affect the way we respond to and come to know that particular town.

This illustration has important parallels with the way children learn and how we relate to that learning and is especially important if we consider it necessary to provide a range and variety of first-hand experience as a vital part of that learning.

First-hand Experience

Only in exceptional circumstances will babies be inhibited from learning through first-hand experience. When circumstances have come to light where a baby has been confined over a long period of time, the sensory deprivation which results is apparent. For example, the confidence with which the baby interacts with the environment can be impaired.

The richness and variety of sensory experience which the baby is able to enjoy builds patterns of understanding and sensory alertness in the mind which act as a deep source from which later association and imagery can be drawn.[5] Experiences of temperature, texture, colour, solidity and so on, found in all kinds of natural and man-made objects, feed the sensory pattern-making as the child grows.

First-hand experience has other characteristics also, those of being able to focus, sharply and intensely, the sensitive energies. A child presented with the actual experience, say, of a live duck will become totally attentive to the experience of duck. Whether this is primarily visual, tactile, auditory or spatial will depend on the child. What is certain is that the memory of the experience can be sharply recalled, not just as shape, colour or texture of duck, but in the particulars of smell and the associations of noises and other aspects of the event. There is a totality of recall involving associations and memories which can never be quite the same when derived from a second-hand experience such as from television or the pictures in books.

We can all recall from our past experience moments when our senses were alerted so significantly that, given time and quiet reflection, we 'summon up remembrance of things past' in the Proustian sense.

Thus, the patterns of sensory understanding which develop as the baby grows through infancy to childhood will be immeasurably enriched through continual first-hand experience.

How such experiences are utilised in educating the child will form part of a later chapter. The point I wish to stress now is their potential to enrich and extend learning and make it more personal. The way in which parents and teachers provide first-hand experiences is obviously important, for it is not just a matter of assuming interest, attention and learning, by taking a child to an exotic location. The way parents and teachers observe children and listen to them in their ordinary environment is crucial if the practised confidence to share revelations is to grow.

One way in which adults can become aware of the way children learn is through their different forms of communication. Words alone can tell us certain things, but need to be accompanied by expression and gesture. Even then, we would miss an enormous amount if we ignored drawing and making things. It is, therefore, necessary to consider the ways in which we communicate.

The Importance of Communication

A newly born baby will communicate with its mother in all kinds of direct and extra-sensory ways. The bonding[6] between mother and baby is more to do with an affinity than a process. However, the baby soon begins to relate to other phenomena in his immediate environment, through hearing, sight and touch. Soon he is generating his own means of contact through making sounds of great variety and expressive quality, through gesture and facial expressions and through handling objects and substances such as food.

Thus, the baby moves into infancy engaging those around him with a range of different means which become gradually more differentiated and elaborated.

Between the isolation of the child, within his own sensory experience (with its ever-present possibility of hurting and frightening as well as soothing and comforting) and the contact with the mother, there exists a gap. This gap continues to widen as the child grows towards independence in mobility and action, but there is the need to bridge it, to establish contact across it. It is in this sense that we return to the second statement by Leboyer 'where the child begins to explore feelings of separateness which are the beginnings of his new life'.

These feelings are there from the moment the child leaves the womb-world of the mother and the physical connection of the cord is cut.

I believe that we use 'media' of various kinds to help us find our way back to some form of integration and some semblance, however fleeting, of unity between outer and inner experience. Media enable us to do this.

Media can be defined as any substances or means which act as a carrier or contact between our understanding, knowledge and responses and those of another.[7] Thus, the infant will use sounds, gestures, facial expressions, objects and substances in order to attract and keep the attention of the mother. These will be 'organised' through the patterns they can support or those which are encouraged by the recipients of the child's communication. In a highly literate society, sounds will soon be formed into or interpreted as words, and words as sentences with meanings. Similarly gestures, at an earlier time than sounds, will be quite explicit as to their intention.

The use of objects and substances, although communicating just as clearly, requires greater observation for us to be able to 'read' them. For just as a child's vocabulary of sounds builds towards verbal communication, so their vocabulary of marks builds towards visual communication, though we seldom look upon it in this way because, in our culture, we do not value visual ideas in the same way that we do words.

The range and variety of means with which an infant is able to explore his/her environment and communicate this visually is considerable. When infants are given the confidence and support through parental or teacher interest and expectation their visual communication can evolve at an enormous pace. Clearly the availability of media and the range of experiences are aspects of this support.

Media

An infant's experience of the world is egocentric, not conceptual; it is direct and spontaneous rather than detached and reflective; it is total, all-embracing of the moment of contact rather than selective or particularised.

The child's use of media mirrors this relationship to experience, and initially is undifferentiated. Sounds, gestures, marks and expressions intermingle to attract and hold the mother's attention. However, as the child grows and contact with the environment widens, so the means of communication become more differentiated and complex. Sounds and words begin to take on the linear form of sentences, objects find their place and relationship to each other and marks begin to resolve in simple, diagrammatic schemes.

It could be argued that any means of bridging the gap between oneself and others, any way of communicating thoughts, feelings and ideas could be labelled a medium. Thus, words and gestures could be called media. However, for the purposes of this book, media will refer to those substances which are able to create visual marks and forms, that is pencil, paint, crayon, clay, paper, fabric and so on; these will be considered further in Chapters 8 and 10.

Babies will explore fabric and foodstuffs in the same open way as crayons or plasticine. The response to these substances will be searching and indiscriminate. Soon, however, the infant will adapt and modify the way in which they are handled. Gradually, patterns of marks can be distinguished where previously there appeared only scribble. As Rhoda Kellogg[8] has shown, there will emerge a number of clearly recognisable kinds of marks or symbols. These will be combined in various ways and become more complex and descriptive of parts or aspects of real things in the child's environment.

Observation of infants will reveal the wide range of expression and communication which is possible through the use of visual media. Many things can be seen in an infant's drawing, painting or modelling which could not easily be communicated in words. Shape, texture, colour and relationship are more readily expressed visually than verbally.

One also has to realise that in order to express them one has to have noticed them. Therefore the expression of visual, tactile and spatial experience reflects the enrichment of the child's pattern of understanding of them.

To sum up, I believe it is essential to consider the development of children prior to the particular age group to be discussed in this book. This leads me to consider certain basic ideas about the nature of learning, particularly in regard to the visual arts. Exploration, control and sensitivity are seen as modes of experience through which learning takes place. The relationship between exploration and control is achieved through sensitivity.

This relationship enables the infant to make increasingly complex and differentiated statements about his/her experience through the use of media. Media are understood to be all those substances which provide the means for visual, tactile and spatial communication. Such communication is as vital to the healthy development of the infant as verbal communication. In order to expand this point, the next chapter considers a broad, developmental scheme for the growth of minds from birth to adolescence.

Notes

1. Frederick Leboyer, *Birth Without Violence* (Wildwood House, 1974).

2. Margaret Donaldson, *Children's Minds* (Fontana, Collins, 1978), ch. 10, p. 111.

3. Daniel Stern, *First Relationship: Infant and Mother* (Fontana, Opea Books, 1977).

4. Lyall Watson, *Life Tide* (Coronet, 1980), p. 51.

5. See Joseph Chilton Pearce, *Magical Child* (Paladin, 1979), p. 11.

6. Ibid., pp. 51-63.

7. See Elliot Eisner, *Educating Artistic Vision* (Collier, Macmillan, 1972), p. 81.

8. Rhoda Kellogg, *Analysing Children's Art* (National Books, 1969).

2 THE SEARCH FOR MEANING: A POSSIBLE DEVELOPMENTAL SCHEMA

Three key points of change in the development of the human mind are considered, particularly for the way they affect the individual's relationship to the world around and their understanding of it. Egocentricity, self-awareness and self-consciousness are seen as vital steps to maturity, each of which is mirrored in the kind of art children produce arising from the changed way they view the world. Each change or natural 'shock' is discussed in relation to developments in children's art because they are seen broadly as the basis and motivation of much of the art that is produced at the different periods of a child's development. Awareness of these changes is considered essential if teachers are to understand how best to help children at different ages.

The following developmental schema is based on the idea that there are three 'shocks' which occur naturally in the growth of the human mind. They are referred to as shocks because they have the effect of causing the mind to respond quite differently to experience; if not immediately, then over a relatively short period of time. The stimulus which arises naturally as part of biological development seems to be essential to the way we learn to survive and the manner in which the mind is able to understand or process experience.

Partly because these shocks are triggered biologically, they promote changes which are long-lasting, dramatic in effect and irreversible. The baby's need to seek stimuli, the infant's development through egocentricity to self-awareness and the self-consciousness of the adolescent are necessary and vital steps to maturity and survival. Each successive development is promoted by significant biological change. Such change may occur at different ages in different people; the birth of most children is after nine months' womb-life; the change from egocentricity to self-awareness is between six and a half and seven and a half years of age; the rise of self-consciousness in puberty is anywhere between the ages of ten and seventeen and seems to be affected by sex and by cultural, social and other factors, such as health and upbringing.

What seems undeniable is that significant change takes place and that this change is largely to do with the way in which the human mind is able and prepared to perceive life's experience in radically different ways. These points of change are evident in the behaviour and communication of children and show up clearly in the art they produce as, for example, in the images which interest or excite them and the ideas which fill their minds.

If it is agreed that significant changes take place at or around these periods in human development, and there is considerable evidence to support this, then the important questions to explore are what is their function and do they have particular significance for creative visual experience?

First, I believe that they are quite different from imposed or man-made changes or shocks such as natural disasters. The shocks to which I refer are part and parcel of growing up and promote positive and necessary change. It is difficult to argue that the change from egocentricity to self-awareness is not both necessary for growth and basically good for survival. Shocks such as the loss of one's mother may seriously inhibit or damage one's growth chances, but will not stop the occurrence of the three natural shocks which I suggest. Furthermore, the three shocks which promote the growth of mind happen to everyone at particular points in their growth.

Could the growth of mind take place without them? I imagine that there is as strong a tendency in all of us to take the easy way, the route of less effort or difficulty, as there is to search for new experience and make fresh endeavours. However, the capacity to form concepts and be self-aware and the heightening of understanding through self-consciousness seem vital to our full maturity as individuals.

Doubtless we would like to remain egocentric if we could get away with it and thus avoid the uncertainties and discomfort of being self-aware. Yet we know that self-awareness brings peculiar satisfactions and rewards and is essential if we are to cope with a wider and more diverse life experience.

So one function of these natural shocks, which can be distinguished, is that they promote change which is necessary and irrevocable. In this sense the growth of mind could not take place without them.

Secondly, a characteristic of these natural shocks seems to be that they impel the mind towards some positive contact and interaction with the world outside itself. When you become self-aware you cannot avoid taking account of things, events and people outside your own private scheme of things. When you are impelled into self-consciousness, you are automatically aware of yourself being what you are in different circumstances. The fact of seeing that it is you who changes as much as others, of being outside your actions but still performing them, is both disturbing but necessary if we are to enable others to live and live satisfactorily ourselves. The effect of appearances and the parallels and metaphors with our own appearance and way of understanding are a significant factor in art experiences. The state of self-consciousness is clearly important at a stage when it is possible to reproduce the species.

Each of these changes which bring us into a different relationship with the world both register in the visual arts and are heightened by the kinds of observations and analogies which making art promotes: in order to make a visual statement about some aspect of our experience the mind focuses on it in particular ways, seeing shapes, colours, surfaces and forms. In communicating these visually, memories are evoked, comparisons made and relationships sharpened.

We may, of course, find all kinds of ways to cover up, disguise and underplay our self-consciousness, but as a means for prolonging our survival it cannot be doubted.

Thirdly, these natural shocks enable quite new and distinct ways of processing and extending experience to arise. Not only are we able to experience the world and its multiplicity of relationships differently, but we are able to build different concepts and working models of it. In this way a child and an adolescent is able to keep in touch with his/her own reality and find personal meaning in it. The visual language of infant schema, childhood ideas or adolescent imagery seems to have this capacity. Through self-consciousness we are also able to be responsible for the development and care of new life, for being conscious of our own responses and thoughts in relation to others is different from just being aware that they are different from us. Such relationships, concepts or models are not worked on formally or abstractly but require a language or medium which enables coherence to be given to them.

Therefore, it does seem that the three natural shocks do have a special function in the growth of the human mind, and that such growth would not occur without them. Furthermore, this function can be seen mirrored in the development of visual ideas at different stages of growth. Let us now examine each of these shocks in more detail as a way of preparing the ground to consider the implications for teaching in general and teaching art in particular.

The First Shock

The first shock occurs at birth when the baby leaves the mother's body and the umbilical cord is cut. No more can it be protected by the enclosed, sensorily quiescent and regulated space of the mother's womb. The baby has to begin to find ways of living a separate existence; an existence which has been separated by the cutting of the umbilical cord.

In other words, the baby is thrust irreversibly into contact with all the sensory stimulus of whatever environment it is born into and it has to find the means to know that world and survive in it.

This is, of course, a necessary and vital step in its development from foetus to infant. If we were marsupials and were able, initially, to develop in our mother's pouch, would the 'shock' of change be as effective? Would our sensory intelligence of the world be developed in the same way?

Perhaps our perceptions of how dramatic this change really is can only come about through dreams, fantasies or approximations which may occur in our lives. When we have a deeply pleasurable experience or are comforted in some way, we may have feelings near those of a child's womb life. An example of the kind of sensation of returning to womb-life experience for some people is the taking of a bath. The slight loss of weight, the warmth and feeling of enclosure and relaxation echo something of the quality of being in the womb.

The French obstetrician, Frederick Leboyer, evolved the method of placing a newly born baby in a bath of blood-heat water for this reason. After nearly thirty years of delivering babies in the traditional western manner, whereby the baby is born into a well lit, clinical environment, the umbilical cord cut immediately and the baby held upside down to clear the lungs, he experienced grave doubts about the rightness of this approach.

He believed that the transition from womb life to outside life should be managed with as little sensory contrast as possible. Dim lights, gentle stroking when the baby is rested on the mother's abdomen and restraint in cutting the umbilicus until it has ceased to pulse, and the placing of the baby in a bath of blood-heat water are all intended to make the transition as smooth and calm as possible. The response of the babies to this approach is remarkably different from that of others brought into a world of harsh light, noise and temperature variation.

This first 'shock' triggers the necessity for the infant to explore the sensations of his own body and his immediate surroundings. He does this by sucking and squeezing, pushing and pulling, thrusting out and withdrawing and so on. Such direct sensory exploration enables the baby to develop a sensory intelligence about the world in which he finds himself and of which he is now a part. This sensory intelligence needs to be fed on sensory experience as much as the baby's body on physical foods.

As Daniel Stern[1] points out, a baby will seek out stimulation and develop a drive for it which is not unlike hunger, for the satisfactions derived from a variety of stimuli are the earliest experiences on which all later understandings will develop.

Daniel Stern further suggests that a baby will soon be stimulated not only by fresh experience but also by the match or mis-match of stimuli to his own developing patterns of understanding. This experience, early in the baby's life, forms the foundation for perceptual, cognitive and sensory-motor skills.

This is a period of rapid growth, with the baby achieving half adult height by the age of three and with the increase in the brain's capacity even more rapid than this. At such times of growth any organism is extremely sensitive to all kinds of influences. Therefore, the patterns laid down in the mind at this time will be very long-lasting and shape the future of the individual in his response to experience and understanding of it. Clearly the quality and variety of experience gained within the security and care of the mother at this time is very important. These experiences, which nourish the baby's growth, are of different kinds, ranging from physical caring and nourishment through various sensory experiences and emotional security and satisfaction.

As the baby grows into and through infancy, so the action and responses to the world around become more complex and differentiated, as is evident, for example, in their drawings, speech and play patterns.

As the infant's capacity to communicate with and manipulate the different elements in his world grows, his/her means of communicating will become more complex and accomplished. The use of the voice, the handling of sounds, gestures and expressions show this, as does the making of marks. The early scribbles soon build a vocabulary of marks which the infant forms into simple diagrammatic images. These develop into more complicated and assured statements about the things which attract and excite him.

Thus the infant will develop a sharper and more atuned response to his world, handle more items of experience and evolve a greater variety of means to do so. Contained in this is an increased knowingness about the world. One could say that the vocabulary of marks, sounds, gestures and facial expressions grows in richness and variety and becomes a potential resource for communication.

This could not have happened if the infant was still physically or metaphorically joined to the mother. The importance and necessity to move about in the world, independently, in order to maintain levels of sensory stimulation, is an increasing factor in the development of the child's mind, showing that separation, with care and security, is essential for development.

As soon as the baby begins to crawl, the need for this sensory stimulus becomes even more evident. At this time, kinaesthetic and spatial experiences are added to those already gained. Moving over, under, through; being within, alongside, on top of; travelling across, between or around are all significant kinaesthetic and spatial experiences that enable the mind to orientate itself to the world and develop a sensory intelligence about it. The manipulation of objects and solid or plastic substances and the use of gesture in mark making with paint and pencil parallel this development.

Egocentricity

The way in which the infant experiences the world is egocentric. The infant can only comprehend the world from his own standpoint — it and all that it contains exists just for him. Such self-centred experience does not compare or evaluate; it cannot conceive alternative views from the one presented or even wholeness where only part is seen. The understanding of the world is as it appears at the moment and exists at that moment for the infant alone.[2] (See Figure 2.1, p. 19.)

The state of egocentricity obviously enables the infant to survive, if in no other sense, by demanding, as far as possible in its circumstances, those things necessary for its happiness, wellbeing and therefore successful development. Egocentricity enables the infant to take and go on taking from the parents, and the world around,

Figure 2.1: Grandpa

This child's experience of Grandpa is shown clearly in his drawing. Grandpa was tall, sometimes he misplaced his feet, especially the thrusting front one, and he walked with his hands behind his back. These parts of grandpa were important and noticed far more than his face. This is an egocentric view of grandpa.

the sensory food necessary for physical survival and emotional and mental development. It is essential that the infant should be able to do this without such 'feeling' being compromised by comparisons, guilt, feelings of greed, concepts of sharing or defering gratification and so on; such states of mind are for a later stage in development! In their drawings there is no compromise with knowing, putting in exact details or getting shapes right. The schematic images express directly the infant's response but also contain a certain knowing. The problems of getting things looking right are, similarly, a part of a later stage.

Yet, the state of egocentricity cannot go on indefinitely, for the individual would acquire a totally distorted view of the world that would ultimately make survival very hazardous and perhaps impossible.

Physical dangers alone, in pursuing one's life with a totally egocentric view, would be enormous. Presumably one would neither understand nor accept rules or regulations, responding only by invitation, training or fear. Such mechanisms would hardly help one to adapt intelligently to circumstances where the rules or conditions varied. In order to understand rules and to follow them one has to have evolved some concept of the game and the part others play in it.

Obviously, one of the steps to maturity is to realise that other people and things do not exist just for you. There is a significant reciprocal way in which each one survives by his understanding of and responsibility for others' survival as well as his own.

Furthermore, to become part of a group, a member of a community, a participant in a society, one has to be able to share values, attitudes and aspirations.

Thus, the protection of the individual mind could not be assured if it remained in the insular, egocentric mode of experiencing, even though such a state of innocence has been longed for by some people. However, a return to the 'Garden of Eden' is impossible after the shock expulsion from the womb. In fact, in order for the next step to be taken in the development of mind, another 'shock' is required. This time it will promote the development of self-awareness.

Before discussing this next stage, it is necessary to refer to some of the findings of research into the development of the human brain over recent years.

In the 1950s Roger Sperry and associates began split-brain

experiments on animals, followed in 1962 by the opportunity to study a man who had had an operation to sever the two sides of his brain, as described by Blakeslee.[3]

It was from this time that observations accumulated of epileptic, schizophrenic and brain-damaged patients and led to the understanding of the different functions of the two halves of the brain. It was found that the left and right hemispheres processed information rather differently; the left in a sequential, analytical and logical manner and the right in broad patterns, images and spatial ways.

In normal development, the differentiation between these hemispheres is not so marked as this might suggest, and both forms of understanding are needed in order to manage the range of experiences involved in living. However, there seems little doubt that the over-emphasis placed on verbal and numerate forms of intelligence does atrophy and spatial, visual and holistic forms.

At birth the two hemispheres are separate and it is during the period of considerable and rapid growth that the hemispheres are joined together by a thick knot of nerves called the Corpus Callosum. On present evidence it seems that the Corpus Callosum is fully formed and able to link the two hemispheres between the ages of six and seven. It is after this time that the different ways of processing information for each hemisphere come into relationship and interaction. It seems a reasonable deduction that what I have called the second 'shock', occurring soon after this time, is intimately linked with this development.

The second shock promotes self-awareness; that is the capacity to see differences and similarities, to compare and distinguish, to question experience and form concepts about it. Almost, the experience of one part of the mind seeing the other! The beginnings of self-doubt and comparisons with others, especially one's own art with that of other children or with reality, stem from this time.

The Second Shock in the Development of Mind

Seven is often referred to as the age of self-awareness. It is the age when there is a curiosity about experience, about things, people, events and places. This leads the child to realise that the way he sees the world and how it actually is are two different things. He also becomes aware that he sees, feels and knows differently from others. He begins to realise, as a notion rather than an action, such things as right and wrong, good and bad, friend and foe, and, of course, correct shape, realness and art that is 'good'.

This is a time when children begin to participate in games, in the sense of following and making up rules. Firm friendships arise which can evolve elaborate codes of behaviour, language, patterns of play and types of art, especially drawing, which are 'best'. In one sentence, the mind is now able to form concepts independently of direct experience. This also means that concepts about how things should look arise and can be derived from many and various sources such as comics, television and older siblings.

This is a profound and far-reaching development and effectively takes the individual out of infancy into childhood. This is a major step in the development of mind which changes, irrevocably, the way in which the world is seen and understood. No longer can the individual behave as if the whole world was made for him. That egocentric 'paradise' will have vanished for ever and even if he behaves like a spoilt child, he will be disturbed by questioning and doubt. He/she may resort to simple schemata in his/her drawing but may doubt their capacity to satisfy the way he/she begins to see the world. (See Figure 2.2, p. 23.)

Now the world suddenly seems immense, the boundaries of experience and of knowing continually roll back; complications seem to arise that cause conflict and uncertainty; many things, previously accepted and enjoyed, now seem incomprehensible. The world is both exciting and worrying, exhilarating and daunting. Things are not as they seem, nor as they have been imagined.

There is, none the less, a fascination with how things work, what makes them behave as they do, whether a machine or a person. Friendships are made and broken, objects taken apart and re-made; there is an investigation and analysis, taking apart and collecting together, re-making and inventing.[4] The child's approach to art clearly demonstrates this development. This becomes the mind's main mode of experience for understanding the world and the many and varied experiences it offers at this time.[5]

In other words, the mind now seeks to make sense of experience rather than just engage sensorily and spontaneously in it. Play becomes something that is talked about and planned and can more often be governed by acquired or improvised rules.

This, I believe, is the significance of the second 'shock'. The

Figure 2.2: Trams

After the second shock in the development of mind (post seven years old) the child is able to conceive other points of view than the immediate, sides, interiors, shapes behind each other and so on. He is able to form concepts about his experience.

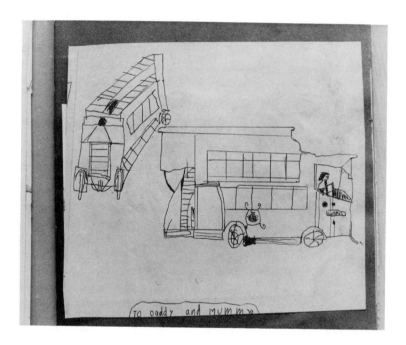

mind is able to engage in experience and stand back from it; able to construct and plan ways of developing action as well as participating in it. The mind has entered a new and important phase, when both hemispheres are beginning to interact; when broad concepts, patterns and relationships can be conceived as well as the sequence, order and logic of their structuring.

Evidence of this change, in the way the mind deals with experience and comes to understand it, is abundant in children's play and in their drawing, to name two examples. (See Figure 2.3, p. 24.)

In play, for instance, whereas the infant would accept any found or given object as the means for developing imaginative play, after the 'shock' at seven he will question the correctness and realness of an object before it is able to satisfy his demands for play. A box

Figure 2.3: X-ray House

This drawing shows evidence of the child handling relationships of shape and relationship in the arrangement of the house as well as sequence and logic in the plumbing and lighting.

used for a car will have to have wheels to enable it to run. A camera made from Lego will have to have a lens and a viewer. When these criteria satisfy his concept of camera, he can then play with it. Should a friend laugh at his pretend Lego camera, then he will either throw it away or invent something else. This shows us how he is influenced by concepts about the world and its objects as well as by the concepts of others.

The range of mental activity thus widens at this time, from pure fantasy to simple technological invention. The potential for learning about the world is likewise increased enormously. It is also at this time that children learn to play the schooling game in whatever way teachers set it up, and, of course, to produce the art teachers seem to like or want. Unfortunately they can also get the idea that they are no good at 'art' and never will be.

Children's drawings are another good example of how the mind copes with experience and processes it, for drawings actually register changes in a child's way of seeing and thinking for us to observe. Yet, how seldom do schools keep any record of children's drawings or even make collections of them for these purposes.

In a series of drawings by one child there is clear evidence that his knowledge about the world begins to interfere with and challenge his accepted response to it. Knowing becomes interposed between his direct, imaginative response and its interpretation in drawing. Reality impresses itself on the child and can become so dominant that it makes him feel increasingly inadequate. The comments and judgements of other children will pressurise this situation, intensifying the child's need to find forms of representation or approximation which are satisfying. In the same way that children will share in games, so they will share ideas for making drawings and the kinds of rules for doing so. Often these can be quite different from those of the teacher or the ones which appear to be acceptable at school.

Children's drawings at this time will reflect all these considerations. There will be the pleasure and security of using existing schemata or demonstrating new discoveries, whether techniques, skills or ways of representing. These will exist alongside the frustration of a lack of skill or knowledge and the feelings of inadequacy.

The teacher has a quite specific and important role to play in these developments, in my view, and this will be explored in Chapters 6 and 7. The point I wish to make here is that the mind has embarked on the next significant phase of its development.

The forming of concepts from our perceptions of the world enables us to interpret any experience rather than accept it at face value. Merely to accept it is to describe it as it appears at any given moment. However, we soon learn that the world is not static but made up of a continually shifting kaleidoscope of impressions and sensations. These do not become significant or comprehensible by being described or annotated. In order for them to have any meaning for us we must develop workable concepts and evolve ideas about them. Making art, drawing, painting, prints, models or whatever else, is an important means for doing this.

In order to make sense from experience we have to relate what we see and experience to our pattern of understanding. Such a pattern is built up over a lifetime from the earliest moments. Whether we realise it consciously or not, such an internalised pattern of understanding is a constant touchstone for every new encounter. We are as much embedded in it as it in us. We bring to each experience that pattern of knowing and responding which is ours and use this to select, discriminate and organise, so that we can understand and cope with it.

The mechanism which children evolve at this time for handling new experience is that of ideas. Ideas stand at the threshold between their understanding pattern and the new experience, enabling them to personalise it and fit it into their scheme of things. I believe that it is through their own ideas that children come to make sense of the world at a time when it seems ever more complicated, expanding and demanding.

However, the true significance of the use of ideas to handle experience for me is that it leads away from the notion of description of that experience towards interpretation of it.[6] Interpretation is a much richer and more potent idea than description, both in its intention and outcome, and is profoundly significant for art education. Let us explore why.

Consciously or otherwise, one might suppose that any description of an experience would be peculiar to the individual making it, as it is bound to contain the particular observations and choices of the individual, whether intended or not. So how is interpretation different? Interpretation requires personal choice of which particular forms of expression are necessary for it to become manifest. The motivation and intention behind making an interpretation are very different from that of description. Whereas description would play down the effects of media where they interfere with representation, interpretation will deliberately account for the qualities of media in the eventual form it takes.

For example, a drawn description of a tree will subordinate the marks of the pencil to elicit as close an approximation to leafiness as possible, and any ambiguity that exists will be through simplification and may even be explained by words or some other means. An interpretation will play with the inherent qualities of the medium to produce a tension or ambiguity between medium and referent, between pencil scribble and leafy tree, between idea and form, between content and its expression.

It is the intention behind interpretation that is quite different from that of description. Whereas description may seek to achieve some kind of explanation through representing or annotating the item observed, interpretation is concerned with specific selection, viewpoint, and especially with personal meaning.

Meaning is not just assumed in the description of an object. Description does not seek to probe or question the significance of an appearance or one's response to it because it does not intend to do so; it merely informs.

Interpretation, on the other hand, questions the nature of the individual's experience of an object as well as the relationship of the object to its position, history, purpose and so on. The notion of interpretation thus takes us beyond that of describing the world or taking it apart to see how it works to make sense of it. Through interpretation we try to come to terms with the experience of the object, whether this is through its function, purpose, or some other aspect. For it is one thing to know how something works or came to be and quite another to realise, personally, its significance or its historical, social or cultural value. It is here that art, like any language, can carry all kinds of 'messages' in its forms, both personal and cultural, apart from its descriptive connotation.

Yet from observation it is apparent that, as children grow through the period between the second and third shocks, they become increasingly interested in and attracted to conceptual and symbolic forms of visual ideas. Paradoxically, although they will assert that they cannot draw and are not interested in art, they will spend time copying certain kinds of images, admiring others which may be derivative stereotypes and according status to their peers who can make passable drawings plagiarised from commercial sources. Films like Star Wars and cartoon characters like Snoopy can generate considerable drawing activity.

One might conclude that there is a keen interest in many visual aspects of the world in which they live, even though this does not always find its place in their expressive, visual vocabulary or the work of schools. If they do not make their own art, it does not mean they are not keenly interested in visual ideas. Perhaps we need to find ways to talk with children about the images which excite them and to establish a vocabulary which helps us to negotiate ideas and meanings with them. In this way the separations and divisions they feel in themselves and in their relationship with the world can find a means of personal negotiation.

This is a time when children will be attracted by visual ideas, many of which will be in the popular idiom. In all kinds of ways, they will borrow, copy, adapt and exchange visual ideas and ways for producing them in order to satisfy their own ends. In one sense this is parallel to them taking things apart to see how they work except that it is with the variety of visual forms with which they are constantly in touch.

The danger is that a child can get stuck in one particular idiom and find it difficult to develop beyond it, or he can feel unable to manage any visual form of communication and easily give up. Here again, the role of the teacher is crucial, in widening and enriching the child's own visual language and giving it a broader context by sharing other cultural and historical forms of art. Widening children's visual horizons is important and this aspect of teaching will be explored more fully in Chapter 7.

During this period of time, from the age of seven to puberty, many other developments will be taking place. The child will be growing considerably even if at a different rate from other children; he or she will be getting taller and filling out, and with these physical changes become more daring and challenging to the world around. Whether boy or girl, he/she will develop new skills and refine others, learn to manage him-/herself in a whole variety of new situations with apparent confidence and greater ease. Particular skills will be developed and knowledge acquired about particular fields of interest. Friendships and relationships to groups will become more dominant features of their experience and colour the way in which they view and interpret the world. (See Figure 2.4, p. 29.)

The difference between maleness and femaleness will become more obvious to each sex, not just in their physical development but in their choice of interests, patterns of social behaviour and way of dealing with the world. Generally speaking, girls mature earlier than boys and this can promote noticeably different attitudes.

Such contradictory feelings as aggression and passivity, the need to challenge and the desire to be cared for will pervade children's experience of growing up at this time. These developments arise from the rapid change in body chemistry taking place during puberty and produce all kinds of contradictory thoughts and unresolved and apparently unresolvable tensions. It is from these developments that the third shock arises and leads to the state of self-consciousness.

The Third Shock in the Development of Mind

Although this next shock does not strictly concern this book it is

Figure 2.4: Faces

This sheet of drawings shows a child exploring the idea of faces through borrowing, copying, adapting and developing certain visual forms. This is an important experience which often goes on at home privately and can seldom be related to the child's visual experience at school.

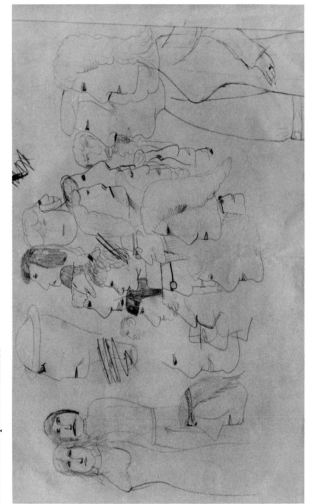

important to mention some of its characteristics as these will illuminate the patterns of behaviour and kinds of understanding evident in children at an earlier stage.

Self-consciousness is a particular condition in which one sees oneself doing things. It is different from self-awareness, which leads one to make comparisons, see differences and similarities without being conscious of one's own shortcomings. Self-awareness helps one to understand relationships and build concepts through processes of selection and discrimination without the added burden of being conscious of one's fallibility or possible lack of understanding to do so.

Self-consciousness is more self-searching and self-revealing and, therefore, disturbing than self-awareness. For example, to be self-conscious one is drawn to see how one's behaviour changes to suit different circumstances. One can see oneself in different guises to suit the changed physical, social and especially emotional context. Going to see Grandma was not just a different experience from going to see a boy or girl friend, but one actually became and could see oneself being a different sort of person.

Thus, the function of the shock of self-consciousness seems to be to make you see yourself as you are or as you pretend to be. This is an important development for the mind which is now able to act to conceive new life. Such a dramatically changed condition as parenthood requires a degree of self-consciousness to be able to cope with the demands, frustrations and responsibilities which it brings.

From the point of view of our discussion, it means that the need to have a satisfying and satisfactory self-image, and to know, even approximately, who you are, are very important and absorbing issues during adolescence. Self-image and identity cannot be achieved easily in a vacuum and this is achieved in relation to others. There is thus a need to experiment with and explore the notions of self-image and identity, whether this is done on ourselves through experimenting with the way we dress and look, or within the context and safety of a group.

There are also those forms of human discourse and expression which deal specifically with images, namely the arts. Having an intelligence about the arts is, in part, being able to read, respond to and understand images. How much more confident and able would young people become in handling their explorations of image making if they had been trusted and encouraged to develop their own visual, interpretive language during the middle years of their childhood.

Here I see a clear connection between the intelligence to understand and interpret the world visually and the necessary skills to manage the shock of self-consciousness and the crisis of identity in adolescence. I see a continuity of need which is all part of the way maturity and adulthood is achieved and I therefore mention it here although it is, strictly speaking, outside the brief of this particular book.

To sum up, it is essential, I believe, for each individual in his own time and in his own way to derive personal meaning from his life experiences. We are driven to do this progressively, as we pass through a number of natural 'shocks' which promote independence from our parents and thrust us into some possibility of conscious maturity.

The degree of maturity we achieve will depend on many factors, one of which is the image we form of ourselves and how this is able to sustain us throughout the many and varied circumstances of our living. All societies produce images of one kind or another which focus their beliefs and aspirations. Young people are susceptible to the power of such images and by action and reaction find their own relationship to them. Art, as a means for forming and exploring personal images, can be and should be a significant part of this process.

The images which a society produces are an important means of identifying self and translating our values and aspirations and those of the communities in which we live. It is also a means to integrate our separate experiences of the world outside with that inside.

Notes

1. Daniel Stern, *The First Relationship: Infant and Mother* (Fontana, Opea Books, 1977).
2. See Ruth Beard, *An Outline of Piaget's Developmental Psychology* (Routledge and Kegan Paul, 1969), p. 9.
3. Thomas Blakeslee, *The Right Brain* (Papermac, 1980), pp. 117-18.
4. See Beard, *Piaget's Developmental Psychology*, p. 83.
5 See Howard Gardner, *Artful Scribbles* (Jill Norman, 1980), pp. 167-8; and Keith Gentle, *Learning Through Drawing* (Association of Art Advisers, 1978).
6. See E.F. Schumacher, *Small is Beautiful* (Abacus, 1974), pp. 66-74; and Bruno Bettelheim, *The Uses of Enchantment* (Vintage, 1977), p. 5.

3   THE CHILD STARTS SCHOOL

Starting school is a demanding time for children which requires thought and care on the part of parents and teachers. Children will communicate as much through their art — especially drawing — as by words at this time. Exploratory play and the development of sensory experience are profoundly important for the basis of learning. Both words and drawing evolve a language through which children can explore the world around them and devise ways of communicating. The way the teacher organises and thinks about the classroom space affects the quality and variety of children's learning. The observation of what children do leads to a deeper understanding of how to help them and how their art develops from simple mark making to more elaborate schemata. In these ways this chapter bases the ideas discussed so far in the context of children starting school.

Starting school is a major event for both child and parent. The child will be subject to many new impressions and sensations, some generated in the home, others to be met for the first time at school. There will be all the preparations for the first day, especially the talk between parents, friends of the family, relations and, of course, other children. New words will enter the vocabulary, or at least take on a new and more personal meaning. Clothes, which may have been reserved for best, or clothes bought specially, will take on a fresh significance.

All these impressions may be modified and 'softened' for some children who have older brothers or sisters or who have attended a playgroup or nursery before starting at the 'proper' school. Nevertheless, the change to a pattern of schooling will form a significant watershed in a child's life which will be full of many new impressions and experiences. (See Figure 3.1, p.33.)

In the first instance it will be a time when the child is apart from the mother, with no immediate opportunity to return to her. A relationship will have to be made with another adult, in 'competition' with other children. Already the child will have been expected to grow up, to do many things for himself, to cope with problems and difficulties and to manage himself physically, emotionally and socially.

Relating to other children, or just being with them, can be a

Figure 3.1: Playing Shops

A child will evolve play according to patterns that he/she can sustain. The collecting and ordering of objects will both satisfy and extend the imaginative needs of play.

major task for many children, although it is a time full of possibilities for learning and rich in sharing alongside others. There is still considerable independence in the way children behave towards one another although they will imitate each other and want to take, almost literally, from one another.

The child will find that other children will take or resist, offer or reject in ways which are quite different from the demands and support of the mother. He will have to accommodate many different experiences of others and find his way into new patterns of relationship and activity. The ways in which things are done, where outdoor clothes are hung, shoes changed, where you sit or play, when it's alright to do one thing and not another, what is fun and what is work, all these patterns of activity and rest will be impressed on the child from those first vital weeks at school.

The security and confidence a child feels in the teacher and the classroom is paramount. It can be seen from these opening remarks that not only are there many new things for a child to 'pick up' but that he/she is in a very sensitive, open or threatened position from which to manage the multiplicity of new sensations.

In this situation the main form of exchange will be words: words from the mother, some carrying simple instructions and admonitions, others with deeper emotional content: words from the teacher, telling, cajoling, accepting, supporting: words from other children, half-expressed but whose import is quickly received.

Although words are the main form of exchange, there will be many other exchanges going on which carry as significant and explicit messages as words at this age. The gestures and movements, the grimace and facial expressions, the tones of voice and the associations will generate patterns of response and learning. Amongst all this activity and rest, coming and going, strangeness and familiarity, there remains, to the child, their personal idiosyncracy, the peculiar experience and sensation which makes up their own, individual pattern of understanding.

Each one of us has his/her own inner pattern of knowing and understanding born of the earliest experiences and shaped by the influences of the language and culture in which we develop. Our perceptions about our world and the values which shape it form the patterns of understanding in which our concepts are embedded. Schooling confirms and extends this process of learning, in some directions more consciously than others.[1] Thus words form a language which is strangely predictive of the kinds of associations and norms of the society of which it is a central part. This can also be said about the development of a child's art.

For example, the place of school in relation to family. The kind of regard in which it is held by the community and the reliance placed on school as a place where children should be. Thus, the way in which school is spoken about carries with it many assumptions as to its value and necessity. Can we imagine children being educated in a society without schools?

Similarly, the kinds of images a child draws and their associations in the child's mind are coloured by the way they are embedded in the society and culture of which the child is a part. Although children the world over will use some similar schemata (simple diagrams) other schemata will arise because of cultural influences as with the choice of subject matter.

Apart from words being a form of exchange when the child starts school, the language of marks available to the child through a variety of media will also be an important form of exchange.

As with words, there needs to have been some early exposure to mark making for the child to feel confident and at ease in using drawing, painting or making, as a vehicle for his/her responses. This is as clear in terms of words as it is with making drawings. A child who has enjoyed using drawing implements will not just have accrued a repertoire of marks (as with words) but also have at hand, so to speak, simple schematic images on which to build and elaborate further experience.

Young children will enjoy the sensation of making marks, whether in food, sand, mud or with stone on concrete, chalk on the ground or a pencil or crayon on paper. The fascination of leaving behind a changed surface can be totally absorbing. However, it requires the confidence of frequent use and the use of the discoveries of earlier exploration for the activity of making marks and drawings to shift towards a 'personal' language.

As the child's mark making develops in variety and content, it begins to contain particular characteristics which are that child's way of doing things and his/her attraction to certain themes or sources of stimulation. This personal language should be recognised by teachers through careful observation as it shows aspects of development in the child's awareness and understanding which are as crucial as the development of words and language.

Exploration

The child's explorations of making marks will show evidence of
different kinds of influences and cannot be ascribed to a naïve
exploratory play with mark-making implements alone. There will
be that repertoire of marks which has arisen from the child's play
which will include a natural pleasure and facility with media such
as pencil; a delight in 'scribbling' and making different patterns
and textures and an apparent awareness of certain aspects of the
appearance of things.

Added to this must be the use of certain symbols which appear
to have universal currency, such as the spoked sun or the 'cabbage'
tree. There will also be other influences coming from the society in
which the child grows up, whether through the use of words to
name objects, the language of stories or the sharing interest of parents, and, of course, the many sources of visual stimulation and
interest in television, books and advertising and in the environment.

All of these influences arise from the child's explorations of
making and using the language of marks. Every venture into the
language of marks can become a means for extending them and
including more and more observations because of them. One can
see, from looking at the drawings produced by a child after a
period of time, the evolution of patterns, whether these are to do
with subject matter, gradually elaborated; ways of doing things
which become more certain and facile or the extending of areas of
interest.

It has already been suggested that the search for new and pleasurable experiences also develops patterns of understanding in the
mind. From this it can be seen that certain kinds of experience and
ways of learning from it can only become possible as they are built
upon earlier experience and its expression. If a child has had only a
limited opportunity to draw, then the capacity of the child's mark-
making will be limited. In this case, the primary need for the child
is to be given the trust and confidence to explore the medium.

It is when making discoveries through the use of a medium that
the child elaborates patterns and makes connections between
things. In fact, there are certain kinds of discoveries that can come
about only because drawing or painting media are being used.

The building up and elaboration of marks on a surface, making
shapes and adding to them are ways of developing an intelligence

about the world around. What is noticed and experienced is named and known through a drawing or painting. The particulars of a shape or details of appearance and colour can all be recorded in a drawing or painting where words may be inadequate to such tasks and perhaps inappropriate.

Thus, the important experiences which affect a child on entering school very often find their expression in a child's art, particularly where drawings and paintings are valued by the teacher and the child is encouraged to talk about them by a sympathetic and interested adult who makes time to listen and observe.

Sensory Experience

The basis for much of the early learning of young children is their sensory experience of objects, phenomena and media. It is from their direct sensory experience that their perceptions and responses will be heightened and feelings of greater confidence to explore new sensations will arise. Each new experience has the potential to enlarge the child's pattern of understanding. The enjoyment of objects is particularly important, for the child can take from them as much or as little as he is able. Size, colour, texture, temperature, weight and plasticity are all aspects of objects which a child can sensorily enjoy. Such objects should not be threatening or overwhelming, nor should they have a sameness and familiarity. The child's repertoire of sensations can be enlarged and enhanced through the range of playthings he is given.

We must all be able to remember a particular toy or object that gave us especial satisfaction or pleasure, even comfort. The range of objects also enables the child's pattern of understanding to be more finely tuned and discriminating. In this way the child is developing an intelligence about objects through his perceptions and responses to them. This sensory awareness and discrimination in a young child is the basis of an intelligence which helps the child to bond to the earth and all the perplexing variety of sensations which life provides.

When one considers a child's sensory experience of phenomena this too is an important way in which a child grows. Temperature, moisture, exposure, closeness, being within, on top of, or under, are all important experiences which enable a child to grow in understanding and confidence in relation to the world around him.

Figure 3.2: Lady

The range of marks seen in this drawing arise from a number of sources: the eyes with their lashes relate to the spoked sun, the broad, looping lines from earlier scribble explorations and the patterned dress from 'observations'.

Enjoyment of the weather, of being outside, in grass, under trees, in light or shade, of moving or resting, crawling or climbing — all these are an important part of the child's learning and are directly sensory in the way they are experienced.

The young child cannot have the awareness or understanding of being under a tree until he is there. The actual sensory experience forms the child's understanding and knowing at that time. In this sense, we can easily deprive a child of chances to learn by not thinking about the way that his learning comes about. This is because as adults we do not need to experience something directly in order to know what it might be like.

It is a common experience that when looking at a young child's drawing one becomes aware of some feature or aspect of something a child has seen to which particular prominence has been given. It is only then that one realises a uniqueness about the way young children see that is peculiarly related to their first-hand experience. (See Figure 3.2, p.38.)

When drawing from imagination, those features which arouse the curiosity or excite the child's interest will be handled in terms of the child's existing schemata and patterns of understanding. For example, a strange beast will still have a human schema for its face and those features which impinge on the child's awareness will be given greatest prominence.

The other important area of sensory experience is that of media. Media could be described as substances or means which are able to give form to sensations, feelings, thoughts and ideas, and transmit these to another. In this sense, words are a medium of communication which is used in different ways for different purposes. Young children will use all kinds of ways to communicate, including sounds as well as words, gestures, movements and marks. For the purposes of the discussions in this book, the word 'media' will refer to the visual and tactile media associated with art. For example, mark-making media such as pencil, crayon, chalks and paint as well as plastic three-dimensional media such as clay, and textured, pliable media such as fabric and thread.

A child needs to have handled media regularly in order to feel confident and at ease using them, for not only will a child's responses and understanding be shaped and developed through their continual contact with media, but as they grow and their experience of the world enlarges, so the possibilities of forming, communicating and sharing their experience will grow correspondingly.

When a child explores any medium there is a large element of play in the activity. Play is never purposeless, as it matches each challenge to the potential of the individual. The 'rules' in play are often arbitrary and changed by the individual according to their needs and capabilities. In this way play never produces failure, though it can always produce and confirm a great deal of learning.[2]

Thus, the element of playfulness as a way of finding out about the limitations and possibilities of any medium is very important.

This notion should be considered together with the belief that the human mind seeks ways to order and control its experience through the making of patterns.

These patterns will take many forms which do not always reveal what kind of connections are being made in the child's understanding. Yet what can be seen from observing children and the things they produce is that discoveries and connections are being made. For some it will be an enjoyment and ordering of colour; for others the development of new marks into their existing schemata; for others the making of patterns or relating observed detail.

Whatever way children gain confidence and skill in their art, their continual exploration of the media they use is fundamental to any development. In fact their handling of media needs to be kept open and enjoyable so that they do not feel frustrated or inhibited by it.

In this context it is important to believe that the human mind seeks order and arrangement and is more satisfied with this than chaos. These are the poles of satisfaction and frustration within which a child explores a medium. There will be many ways in which we can see evidence of order being imposed on, or evolved from, handling a medium. Young children (five to seven) will enjoy the physical sensation of the medium and find satisfaction in this alone; others will have a story to tell, changing a drawing or painting as it unfolds with the result often appearing muddled and overworked. Yet others will make shapes and repeat patterns as a way of controlling the medium.

Whatever way a child uses the medium, it is important that he feels confident to really enjoy it and become immersed in handling it. That is, children need to have a time, however brief or long, when they handle the medium in an open, exploratory and free way. How the child is given confidence to do this, and the way in which greater control and understanding are achieved, requires the sensitive, unobtrusive support of an adult. This kind of immersed exploration of media is vital to a child's confident handling of it. One personal observation or response by a child is worth any amount of instruction.

As a child's own mark making evolves, it does so on the basis of the repertoire of marks, schemata and observations already made. Unless a child has a store of visual language available, each new experience can only be met by an inadequate and limiting response. (See Figure 3.3, p.41.)

Figure 3.3: Scribbles

The evolution of mark making starts from simple scribbles from which diagrammatic and symbolic shapes and simple images emerge. These shapes and images become increasingly complex as the child matures.

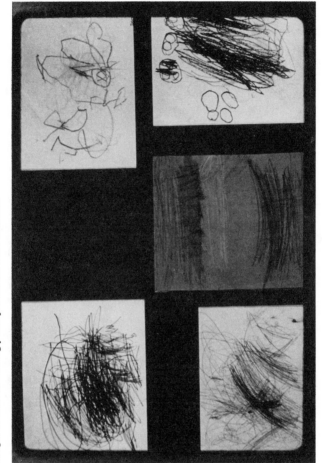

This can be observed in simple things, for if the basic symbols for the figure are not managed, all the richness of clothes, features, actions and situations cannot be manifest in the drawings, paintings or models a child undertakes. New experience, such as the sighting of a helicopter or a wedding dress, would find an inadequate expression if the child's means of communication were limited.

Therefore, the building up of a child's visual vocabulary, both in the choice and enjoyment of different media and the quality of sharing and enjoying looking, is vital. One would say exactly the same about a child's verbal development, with which the visual vocabulary is closely interwoven. For the use of words to name objects is an important way of building patterns of knowing and understanding from which later concepts and interpretations will arise.[3]

An important distinction must be made between words and drawings. Words name things and can stand for them as an abstract, general idea rather than a particular experience. Drawings relate far more to the individual's perception of the actual thing observed. Thus, words can stand between an object and the individual perception of it, but drawings focus individual attention on the features of the object and the way it is seen or has been seen by some other person. We must be alert to the difference between sharing words about an object and actually sharing the object: between expecting a child to handle words as a means of heightening awareness of the object or using drawing as a way of relating personally and particularly to it.

When a child starts school, there are many new experiences and sensations in which he will be involved. The sense of security he feels will promote the confidence to explore, through which learning and understanding will take place.

It is vital for the teacher to have an awareness of the function of drawing and other visual forms of expression as well as literacy and numeracy in order to help the child relate fully to experience and communicate it.

Implications for Teaching

Much could be said about the ways of receiving children into school, but these apply to any area of the child's learning. What seems more appropriate is to consider the thoughts which arise from the discussion so far.

Although the first impressions a child has of school could be confused and bewildering, he soon picks up the signals and gets the idea of what is expected of him from other children as well as the teacher. There has to be a clearly recognised way of doing many of the routine things necessary for the ease of maintenance and smooth running of a school or classroom. Young children can be easily disturbed by too much change, by disorganised and thoughtless handling of such things as changing activities or finding apparatus. Those routines which enable a settled and orderly atmosphere to exist are obviously important to attend to and for children to understand.

The different spaces in a classroom or nursery can be clearly identified: those for exploring tactile media such as sand, water and clay; those for the basic painting or box building; those for table top activities requiring sitting; and so on. Yet, not all these spaces will remain the same and static, for different apparatus can be set out occasionally, different displays of objects to enjoy, a different emphasis in looking or touching, a seasonal feeling and so on.

The learning space can thus have elements of security and familiarity as well as change, variety and stimulation. The teacher will have to work out the most satisfactory way to achieve a balance within the constraints of other demands. As the discussions on teaching arise in each part of this book, a firmer idea of teaching will evolve. At present, the foregoing remarks are made to introduce the teacher's responsibilities with regard to children's exploration of media, for it is as important for a teacher to recognise the need to make exploration purposeful as it is to provide the means for it to take place.

The first essential is that any medium should be clean and well presented. This is not just a fad but has a number of important functions in the way the child comes to terms with media. The child needs to experience the medium as it is, unadulterated and fresh, so that any changes or modifications in texture, form, colour and appearance will register. It is the quality of the experience that is important; the results and the learning will follow automatically if this is right.

Further, the child will respond differently to a well-presented medium and this will be reflected in the work he does. If the teacher's task is to raise levels of interaction and sensitivity, then an obvious start is the way the room, objects in it and different media are cared for and presented. Last, but by no means least, the child can be expected to clear up and leave materials in a clean and reasonable state when he has finished using them. This is all part of the good management of a class and has its spin-off in the attitude of children to their own and other children's work.

Secondly, it is essential to think about the reasons for presenting children with different media to explore, and to have considered what one imagines could be discovered. Although one should not be didactic about this, it does mean that there are certain experiences which one feels it is important to place before children. We know that it is not a matter of the teacher looking for or demanding certain features in a child's art. There must be an alert, well-observed and thereby sensitive exchange going on between the child, what he is doing, and the teacher, from which both child and teacher become more alert to the qualities in a piece of work and the potential for further experience.

Therefore, it seems sensible for the teacher to make specific choices of media and at times to effect certain limitations in the way they are presented, rather than provide too wide a range. There are no absolutes in the way one provides media for children to use, but there must be common sense which both helps the child to find his/her way and enables the teacher to provide variety and quality within the scope of available time, money and resources. The basic aim is to enrich the child's sense of intelligence about the world in which he is growing up and help him to communicate this by one means or another. For example, the sand tray should not become a forsaken part of the classroom, but, through the teacher's observation, it can help children to enjoy and explore the properties of sand, whether wet or dry. Thus moulding, tunnelling, shaping, piling and impressing wet sand would require different objects from the free flowing dry sand. Sand that is too wet or not quite dry can be frustrating rather than satisfying. The way in which objects are added or taken away and the conversations which sand play promotes are the result of observations and insight on the part of the teacher.

Powder paint which is dirty or lumpy can create more problems in mixing, yet children should be given the opportunity to mix paint, to explore its tactile and runny qualities and discover the excitement of making their own colours. Clean powder colour is essential, and a range of colours that is not too wide as to be confusing. Sometimes painting with a few colours is more appropriate and provides greater incentive than having many.

The judgement of the teacher is crucial — not just the judgement, but the way in which the teacher talks to the children about their painting and the qualities which can be found in it. This judgement comes about as much by thinking through what you hope a child will gain from any experience as providing the experience as such. Then, when it is set up, continued, if intermittent, observation by the teacher is important.

Thirdly, it is essential to help children choose appropriate media for the job in hand. Each medium has its own peculiar qualities and these can relate more readily to some ideas than others and to some ways of working than others, to some experiences than others. The teacher can encourage intelligent choice by the value placed on choosing. If he never discusses choosing or the effects of good choice, then this important yet simple aspect of using media will cease to have significance for children.

To help children explore in a purposeful way, the teacher needs to observe children working and support his own observations by discussion with colleagues and reading the studies which have been made by other people. This will provide a teacher with a strong basis of understanding from which he can positively help children to develop their skills, awareness and sensitivity through their art.

Development in Art

All children will use schemata or simple diagrammatic solutions to visual problems. In the age group under consideration in this chapter (three- to seven-year-olds) these will be much in evidence. Sometimes a simple schema will be used when the child is wrestling with a particular idea or conveying something about a particular experience or object. In these circumstances it could seem that the child has regressed in the way he draws but it may only be that other concerns fill the moment.

A child wishing to make a visual statement about an exciting or special event is very likely to resort to schematic elements as props for the more special things he/she wants to communicate. Thus, a well observed vintage car can have a simple schematic driver, or a magnificent bride's dress, well observed in certain particulars, could still have a very simple schematic bride.

Before the age of seven, a child's experience of the world is egocentric. What children know and understand about the world is centred on the self and they have no concept of the world or the objects that fill it independently from their direct experience of it. It follows that a child's way of seeing and understanding will be dictated by his immediate experience and the store of memories and schematic ideas which he evolves.

In this way a child's drawing, paintings and models will often capture something of the essence of an object because the way children respond to it, and the particular aspects to which they are attracted form the substance of their art. There is no independent knowing about the objects which is separate from this direct response. Different elements of the same object or event can appear altogether and in the wrong relationships. One is not made aware of the object or the dominance of its appearance; rather it is the child's mark making and schematic resources which stand out together with a highly idiosyncratic response to the thing depicted. (See Figure 3.4, p.47.)

Is it sufficient to just accept any schematic approximation which a child may use?

It would seem a heresy to suggest that the art which children produce between the ages of five and seven could be better or show improvement. And yet, from one school to another it is possible to see considerable changes and differences in certain aspects of children's art and these are more generally evident across all children. Such elements as the range of things depicted, the quality of mark in a variety of materials and the evidence of first-hand looking will be more apparent in the art of children in one school than another. If this is so, it indicates that we must do more than just accept whatever children produce. The encouragement to enjoy looking at things and responding through the use of mark-making media leads to a greater awareness and confidence in children. Yet, we should never dictate what they do or how they do it as this would tighten up their response and their confidence to communicate it. (See Figure 3.5, p.48.)

The key seems to be in the way first-hand experiences are provided and the way that the teacher affords time to talk and share with children the things they see and do.

The teacher needs to be aware of each child's own idiom of marks and ways of working. In parallel with the mannerisms and

Figure 3.4: Guinea Pigs

The soft chalkiness of pastel and conté crayon made it possible for these children to express something of the textural qualities of the guinea pigs in their drawings.

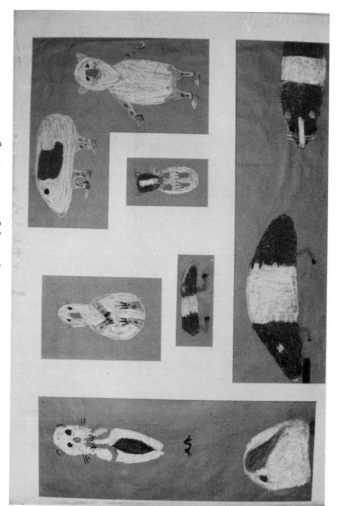

Figure 3.5: Cow

Why is the cow so anxious? Perhaps because there are parts of her which don't fit, like the cat's ears and the knees. These have not been seen directly and are made up from other, casual looking. Other parts show evidence of the child's having really seen a cow, such as the cloven hooves and the nostrils. This indicates that seeing is very particular and requires attention.

use of words and gestures which express something of a child's personality, one can see characteristic ways of working, types of mark and areas of interest. These can be talked about by the teacher and shared with the child, thus reinforcing strengths and confidence. The visual media are so varied in their potential that a given group of children will relate in quite different ways to particular media. Therefore, the choice and opportunity for some children to work for sustained periods with one medium is an important way in which the teacher can help a child's art work to develop. Continually moving to new or different media is not necessary for many children, and the reasons for doing so should be worked out clearly.

Through sharing the art children produce, either one to one or in the group, it is possible to focus on particular elements which occur in it. The way something has been noticed, the handling of a medium, the use of space on paper, the textural quality and so on are all aspects which could be brought out when looking at children's art. It is not that one is forcing the child to produce effects for which they have no understanding or cannot conceptualise, rather it is heightening the shared enjoyment of certain aspects which the child has brought into his work.

Such observation of children making art is necessary if their development is to be valued rather than assumed, for we have to ask whether they would not do as well out of school as in it. There must be particular things which a teacher, in his/her classroom, can offer children that enrich, illuminate, reinforce and extend their experience, and therefore learning, which are different in quality and perhaps kind from those the child meets out of school.

One obvious way in which every teacher can strengthen his/her understanding of children's development and the arguments for the way they see it is by keeping examples of each child's drawing. From such a record it will be possible to see changes and developments which show how the child's intelligence about the world and his awareness of its qualities and properties are progressing. (See Figure 3.6, p.50.)

Such developments would include greater complexity in the way images are made and extended, in the shapes, the things that fill them or surround them, in the relationships of shapes and their placing on the paper. The details, connections and positioning of the things drawn will mark developments in seeing and understanding. Perhaps a booklet set aside for drawing would provide such a record, into which pieces could be stuck and others drawn directly.

In this way a teacher could see the effect of a new stimulus or change of medium and readily show parents or colleagues how a child's understanding of the world was becoming more informed and aware.

To summarise; starting school is one of the most significant events in all our lives. How preparations are made for this affects the first responses. Schools transmit strong cultural influences, which are embedded in systems of education, and children learn, from an early age, to fit into them.

The exploring and controlling of different art media at the early

Figure 3.6: Elephant

The face on this elephant shows how a child will resort to a simple schema to complete a drawing because the most important aspect for him is the mass and texture of the elephant.

stages is profoundly important and contributes to all round confidence, particularly in building up a mark-making vocabulary. Words and marks have different functions although there is a strong parallel in how they are established and both are necessary. A basis of rich, sensory experience is essential to this growth and stimulates the development of these languages.

The teacher has a clear responsibility in relation to children's purposeful enjoyment of media and the quality and variety of environment presented in the classroom. The care of media, observation of children handling them and the presentation of appropriate choices are all aspects of the teacher's work aimed at raising levels of sensitivity and intelligence about visual and aesthetic matters.

Teachers should learn to talk with children about their art and share their responses and ideas. Finding ways of recording and keeping collections of children's work helps in this respect. (See Figure 3.7, p.51.)

Figure 3.7: Hamster and Zebra

These two drawings show something of the development one can look for in a young child's drawing. The hamster is a free flowing scribble with other squiggles and dots almost randomly placed. The zebra shows the child responding to stripiness and the head and eyes are more appropriately placed.

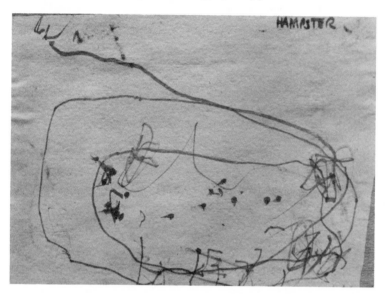

Notes

1. See Eliot Eisner, *Educating Artistic Vision* (Collier, Macmillan, 1972), p.57.

2. See J.C. Pearce, *Magical Child* (Paladin, 1979), p. 142.

3. See Eisner, *Artistic Vision*, p.101.

4 ENRICHING AND EXTENDING THE CHILD'S EXPERIENCE

Children need to build on their understandings and develop them into new experiences. It is argued that the main purpose of the teacher's work with young children is to extend and enrich their sensory experience. As children grow in confidence their handling of materials and enjoyment and understanding of real things will become more involved, complex and knowing. Descriptions are given suggesting how the teacher might think about art materials as a means to enrich children's experiences.

The enjoyment of art materials and the way ideas grow from handling them develops the discussion further and relates it to the needs of older children. Extending simple experiences into new activities and discoveries in collaboration with children is fundamental to the teacher's role. The matrix of provision which enables children's creative activities to grow is discussed as is the way in which it can be used effectively. This chapter and the following one prepare the ground for the discussion of teaching in art in chapter six.

Children have a natural curiosity and like to touch and hold things, to manipulate them and include them in their play. A child without playthings of some kind is a deprived child. Where there are few bought toys, children become very adept at improvising playthings from the most unlikely sources, so strong is the need for exploratory play. As Daniel Stern comments, 'the seeking of stimulation achieves the status of a drive or motivational tendency not unlike that of hunger'.[1] Unfortunately, competition from commercial products can often inhibit the kind of play which thrives on improvisation and inventiveness by overprescribing results or encouraging the child in a desire to be entertained. Therefore, careful selection and presentation of materials and stimuli by an adult, whether parent or teacher, is of great importance if children's sensory experience is to be enriched. The adult's perceptions of how children handle and develop sensory experience is a crucial factor in such selection (See Figure 4.1, p.54.)

Young children between five and seven are developing finer and

Figure 4.1: Sand Play

The child shapes the sand according to his ideas for imaginative play but the sand behaves like sand and thereby shapes and modifies his ideas. This two-way process is found in the use of any material.

finer motor skills enabling them to manipulate quite small and delicate objects, for example connecting blocks and wheels, small brushes and pens, scissors and large needles. It is revealing to note how children's toys have changed over the years from being simple models with applied or cast details to those with moveable parts which can be opened or taken off. The commercial market seems to recognise and exploit children's interests in this direction, producing a wide range of manipulative opportunities in the more expensive toys produced.

The continual availability of different kinds of play materials to extend the child's skills is significant because such skills should never be seen in isolation from the thought process and understandings which they engender. As children's understanding and experience grows their fingers can pick and choose, turn and twiddle, push and pull, prod and squeeze with increasing dexterity. If they are given the chance at home, they will 'be into' everything helping with the cooking and gardening, wanting to take part in any building and making. However, a wise teacher or parent will not permit any and every kind of material and experience, knowing some to be dangerous, others frustrating, and realising that there is often more to be gained by the mastery of a few things, enabling the child to develop his understanding and imaginative play, than the continual moving from one thing to another. Careful choice can help each experience to be rewarding and positive thus building the child's confidence and extending the range of activity as seems appropriate.

Young children's efforts will not be very accomplished nor well sustained but the curiosity will be there impelling them to try and their fingers will probe and manipulate leading the mind into ever richer association with the world around them. As Dr Bronowski wrote about his grandchild in *The Ascent of Man*, 'the march of man is the refinement of the hand in action'.[2] This seems particularly true and apt of children at this time.

Of course there will be many children who will not have the understanding and patience of parents or older siblings to encourage them to explore and learn in this way. They will experience restrictions and frustration, whether this comes about through a home that must not be spoilt or one that doesn't care. Even in these circumstances, given the chance, a child will find some space, some corner of his environment in which to play, where he can begin to manipulate the objects and materials of his environment to create his own pattern of understanding and a world of the imagination. How much more could a child do with the sympathetic understanding and support of a perceptive adult? Places and people must be invented, battles fought, monsters overcome and adventures undertaken. It is a very frightened, sick or apathetic child who does not become involved in such play, and it is play which is stimulated in all kinds of ways, not least by objects and materials, and, of course, by words and activities. A child's play can create a world, for however brief a time, in which he makes the rules and always wins; in which he can feel secure and confident to play out his experiences of the real world around him. The enrichment of play is one of the most significant teaching jobs that a parent or teacher can do but it requires the knowledge gained from the careful observation of children and an acceptance of their level of activity.

How different it is for most children who experience the pressures of having to grow up and come to terms with formal learning, increasingly leaving behind any opportunity to play, to explore in their own way and own time or to follow through their own ideas and investigations. It may well be that many adults who reflect on their lives will recall that somewhere between five and seven they felt they lost something of the magic of childhood, that they had to grow up, take responsibility and somehow lose that innocent and timeless wonder of childhood where so many things seemed to be waiting to be discovered. Of course, seven and eight is a time when children who are happy and confident will want to take responsibility, will want to do things for themselves and imitate the way grown-ups do them. Yet they are still very much children who need the comfort of a lap under them or an arm around them. They can be seen 'regressing', wanting to play with toys and experience the comforts and pleasures of a younger age as well as reaching out into the world of adults.

The adults in their lives become exceptionally important both as models, in terms of interests and expectations, and as the means to further experience. For example, the child who likes clothes and dressing up, or cars and playing with mechanical things, can have such interests extended and enriched through the activity and sharing of his/her parents.

Apart from the verbal exchanges of children during this time their drawings and paintings reveal all the flux and change of patterns of growth or privation. Their drawings can show imaginative leaps, both in what is noticed and understood. Their drawings will reveal things they have seen and we have missed; viewpoints, details, relationships, the peculiarities of dress or expression. The pattern of drawing will not be consistent and at different times will show both development and regression in the kinds of schemata used. At one time the challenge of a new material or experience will draw on all their resources; at another they will resort to more mundane and simple symbolism in order to record an event which was more to do with an unfolding of experience than a strong visual response. (See Figure 4.2, p.57.)

In either case the discussion, questions and appreciation of a teacher who tunes into the child's experience, is significant in helping a child to derive understanding and meaning from the encounter and to explore ways to interpret it verbally and visually. This aspect of teaching is significant in how it helps to extend and enrich the child's art. On one level it is just taking an interest in the child's view of the world; on another it might lead towards new and exciting revelations. In both cases an adult can engender an attitude which promotes sharing and finds such activity rewarding.

What kind of environment do children need at school, from infancy through to junior school, that is going to build on and

Figure 4.2: Birds

The beaks and hanging feet of these gulls have been noticed particularly by the child so that they become a significant feature in his drawing.

enrich this kind of growth? The growth of the child cannot be separated from the conditions in which it takes place.

Although children of infant age are still self-centred in the way they learn about the world around them and relate to others, it is a time when they are beginning to experience the social interaction with other children outside the family in the ordered, particular environment of the school away from home. In the institutional and general spaces of school, having a classroom base, feeling that there is a place to keep your little possessions is important. It is somewhere to return to amongst the bustle of school.

The teacher, as a parent surrogate, is most important, for it is from him/her that the lead will come for the way to behave and what to do, what is valued and what is dismissed. There is bound to be a period of adjustment on coming into school which is helped by a well ordered, calm environment. Some children will need more attention than others, some more encouragement, and so on.

All of these things will be embedded in the quality of the environment, where the child feels wanted but also able to participate. The appearance of the room will make the first impact. The scale and arrangement of furniture, the spaces created and the interesting things to see. It is hard and perhaps unnecessary to separate one aspect of a child's experience from another at this age, but in terms of the discussions in this book, focus will be placed on opportunities for sensory exploration that can extend and enrich the child's capacity to learn.

Possibilities for sensory experience should be provided in the classroom, but not in a haphazard or indifferent way, if children are to gain from enjoying them. This being so, the way in which different kinds of sensory experience are provided, changed or occasionally made available is very important. Some children will apparently need the experience of certain kinds of materials continually, returning to them every day, such as time spent in the sand tray or with building blocks. This occurs with older children also even though they may have reservations about indulging themselves. For example, one eleven-year-old boy I knew worked with clay for some part of almost every day and other children appreciated his skill with the medium and he corresponded with them through it. The need to have his fingers in clay for at least part of most days was understood and allowed for by his teacher.

There are some materials and objects which seem so fundamental to a child's sensory growth that it would seem extraordinary if an infant classroom were not to have them. The basic earthy kind of experiences of water, sand and clay seem absolutely essential as they represent different stages of matter, yet the experiences children have of these materials are often taken for granted while the teacher gets on with number and language work. If a child naturally spends time playing with these basic materials they must have educational potential and be worth a closer study and thought by the teacher.

If water is considered as a material its potential for valuable learning experience becomes apparent. Water flows, settles, makes things damp, runs and bubbles. You can see your breath bubbling down a tube into it or frothing in soap suds. Things float or sink, fill up or drain out; you can colour it and see the light through it, splash and dribble it. Although a child may have experienced water many times, the fact of its being provided in a transparent bath with all kinds of things to try out in and with it focuses the child's awareness on water as a substance. Here, in these simple experiences, are the beginnings of scientific enquiry, the language for discussing and comparing, the observations which stimulate the memory and aesthetic expression.

Water can be enjoyed in so many ways; it can impose itself on the child by not behaving as he expected, or he can impose himself on it by doing again something that he has found out. He can control water because he has explored it and through this he learns to be more alert and aware of the sensations it produces.

Games and experiments with water can become more inventive and complex as the child gets older, but the kind of learning which enters the child's pattern of understanding at this age is an important foundation for later learning. So it is with other earth materials such as sand and clay.

A child's play shapes what the material can offer as much as the material predicts what the child can experience. This two-way exchange is essential to learning, yet requires an openness and confidence from the child which may start as freedom to do anything but be modified by the realisation that anything cannot be done. It is here that important learning takes place and can be witnessed by the observant teacher. Working within the discovered limits of a material is as important as finding out that it runs or sticks in unexpected ways. The teacher's observations, comments, questions and ways of sharing a child's experience help the experience to become more important and more readily communicated, whether this is through the child's words, actions or collaboration with the teacher.

What counts is how the teacher thinks through the purpose of having such materials in the classroom and how he observes and questions their use. Play is potentially one of the greatest ways of learning but it can so easily remain formless and lack development or personal satisfaction and challenge, subsiding into vague therapy or time-filling.

It is important for the teacher to witness children's play, from time to time over a period of time, as it embodies patterns of activity and non-activity and rhythms of learning that are peculiar and essential to the learner. (See Figure 4.3, p.60.) In older children, the manner in which they weigh up situations, visualise possibilities, make connections and work out approaches to problems relates very strongly to play patterns. There are many ways of coming to terms with the creative act, actively manipulating

Figure 4.3: Baby Playing with Bricks

Through play, children are able to build all kinds of understandings about the world around them. Creating order and arrangement with things is one way in which we can see this happening.

materials may be one; sitting still and apparently avoiding contact with the problem may be another. If children are always forced by time and the need for specified results into busyness and pre-scribed or stereotyped learning activity, their confidence and capacity for personal response will be damaged. This is particularly so in art. I believe this to be true for older children also though they become more adept at disguising the effect this has on them.

Therefore, there is much that a teacher can do to enrich chil-dren's play and learning, through the choice and preparation of materials, the way they are presented, added to, discussed, and through the observations, questions and sharing which take place.

For example, clay is another earth material which most children enjoy handling but one which requires the thought and care of the teacher in how it is managed. Clay has certain characteristics which sand and water do not have and it has enormous potential for learning. Clay is, of course, an important medium for the artist and craftsman. It has plasticity and can be moulded and formed; it is three dimensional and can be used to make constructions and build forms and it is expressive, holding the least impression on its surface. Clay continually changes as it is handled, drying out and losing its plasticity, and it can be baked or fired to give it greater permanence.

It is because of this versatility that clay offers so much to children but it must be kept in good heart and presented in good condition for children to use (see Chapter 10). Clay can be formed and shaped, poked and pinched, imprinted and flattened, it can be bored with a finger and made into enclosures and environments, piled up or spread around. The variations clay offers for children's exploration are endless and there is always something that it won't do but just might.

As children develop through the years between eight and early puberty they become fascinated with the world around them and want to investigate and analyse it. Their capacity to form concepts and working ideas about many of the things they see and experience becomes evident in their work with materials and the ideas they want to express through them. Taking apart and re-assembling, separating and analysing different parts and inventing new possibilities, whether in reality or fantasy, becomes a significant mode of learning at this time.

These changes bring with them the desire for more knowledge of the world and the need to evolve techniques for handling it. Children of this age can develop sophisticated ways of handling materials and tools and thinking about ideas. I remember watching two boys of eleven using clay to make a large portrait bust. The head and shoulders were roughed in and joined collaboratively. Then, with consummate ease, one worked on shaping the forms of the head while the other used his own clay-scraping method to create hair for the eyebrows and scalp.

It is clear that children can absorb a considerable amount of learning through the catalyst of their own ideas. This is because their ideas grow out of previous real experience and any understanding arises from their own pattern of knowing and can be related to further experience. Thus they can both generate techniques and ways of working appropriate to the tasks in hand or problems to be solved and absorb techniques they are shown. In handling clay, methods of joining and building are examples of this kind of knowledge and technical understanding. The danger lies in the teacher's making the assumption that children want or need to learn techniques before they can express their ideas properly. The teaching of technique must arise from the observation of the whole of the creative endeavour of the child and not in isolation from other parts of it (see Chapter 6).

One of the most valuable indicators of a child's developing ability to handle ideas and build concepts from his/her experience is the drawings he/she makes. Drawing is a significant form of communication through which children tell us about their experience of the world. A child who may have an only limited verbal vocabulary can have evolved a vocabulary of marks that enables him to communicate a great deal about his experience, what he sees, how he relates to it and to other experiences, and how he is able to understand and think about it. Drawing, by its nature, is able to convey many things about our experience more readily than words. For example, a feeling for shape and pattern, importance through position and scale, the relationship of one thing to another, the texture and density of surfaces and so on. All of these can be conveyed through drawing where words are inadequate. Not only this but also the perceptions of these qualities and distinctions are sharpened through the act of drawing. (See Figure 4.4, p.64.)

Therefore the way in which a teacher talks about children's drawings and shares them is crucial. Different drawing media enable quite distinct responses to be made: the softness of chalk or charcoal; the wiriness or spikiness of pen and ink; the textured waxiness of crayon. These qualities of media themselves can help children to respond to see differently. They can evoke all kinds of images by the way they are used and many children will enjoy the sensation of handling drawing materials whether they make a 'picture' or not. It is important that the teacher helps children to develop their confidence based on the effects and qualities of media as this leads them towards appreciating visual and aesthetic ideas rather than seeing drawing or painting as a poor representation of the real world. (See Figure 4.5, p. 65.)

The teacher can relate the qualities of different drawing materials to the qualities of specific objects and natural forms. This will lead children to make considered choices and think about the effects which media can create. An essential aspect of the teacher's work is to build up an intelligence, in the children, about the materials they use and evolve with them a vocabulary with which to discuss their work. Both of these aspects are essential to the enrichment of children's understanding of art and the extension of their own art experience.

It is necessary to help children to become immersed in handling a material in order to find out what it can do, how it resists or responds to their efforts to manipulate or shape it. This activity has to be free yet requires close attention, for it can be joyous but soon become purposeless. Guidance, help, discussion and above all trust are required from the teacher if children are to derive real value from the exploration of materials. Any material or medium needs to be discovered in a personal way by the individual intending to use it. Where this experience is atrophied, or missed out altogether, the work of the individual suffers. It can become tight, stereotyped, lacking in spontaneity and freshness, and the magic and joy of creating with a material can disappear. For example, paint, as a substance, has an enormous range of behaviour but can be reduced to merely filling in. Paint can run and spread, be built up and added to; it has texture and substance, brilliance and opacity, will mix in all kinds of ways. There is a continual richness of experience and association to be found through the handling of paint which can be entirely forfeited because children are not helped to see and experience it but try only to ape reality in the images they produce.

The type and quality of paint matters as each kind performs differently. The size of brushes, kind of paper, cleanliness of water and so on all make the difference between continued confidence and frustration.

Older children (say between ten and thirteen) can become very inhibited when using paint. They can feel that it is impossible to achieve the realism and detail they see in the world around them. In this case it is necessary to keep their views open and receptive to a variety of ways of working and different kinds of imagery. They will find all sorts of visual models attractive, many of which will be beyond their capability to reproduce. Nevertheless, discussion of these and their own work, bringing out the nature of imagery and the effects of materials and different ways of handling them, can

Figure 4.4: Three Vehicles

In these three drawings one can see a refinement and greater awareness of shape; an understanding of proportion developing and the increase in detail. The second drawing is a developed schema whereas the others show a greater response to observation. a: 3.5 years; b: 4.3 years; c: 4.10 years.

a

b

c

Figure 4.5: Climbing Trees and Helicopter

These drawings show the capacity of drawing to convey such things as shape, texture, pattern, relationship and scale, all experiences and concepts which are much more difficult to handle with words. In the second drawing the medium, thick pencil, has a crucial effect on the visual and aesthetic quality of the work.

extend their ideas and concepts. Of course it is important that materials and media are kept and presented in good order.

Sometimes a simple technique shown to a child or a group at the opportune time will open up new possibilities and provide sufficient confidence for their direction and ideas to be rekindled. At another moment it may be necessary to allow time and space for experiment and investigation into the qualities and effects of paint. I remember several instances when children who found difficulty with painting were able to open up a whole new approach through timely experimentation. An extreme case was one boy of eleven who rolled a marble through paint to achieve his paintings. He soon found that the texture and colour of the paint mattered and had to be carefully controlled to achieve the effects he sought. This experience was unique to him but does show the value in the teacher's being able to support a child in his own researches and finding appropriate ways of looking at and discussing the effects achieved. The relationships between ideas, techniques and teaching will be further explored in Chapter 6. In my view it is essential for a teacher to have thought about these relationships as they are manifest in their own teaching if they are to find ways of enriching and extending the work in art of their pupils. (See Figure 4.6, p.67.)

It can be seen from these comments that the kind of thought and observation which goes into providing some of the basic materials and seeing that they are in good order can generate a lively and purposeful exchange between the child's ideas, the material and the teacher. The same is true when considering the rest of the environment of the classroom which should offer different and varying kinds of stimulus and opportunity for children to explore. It becomes dynamic as opposed to static, when children begin actively to enjoy and participate in it. This will arise through the teacher's watching, listening to and finding ways of sharing children's experiences so that they can be enriched and extended with subtlety and understanding.

A classroom cannot be dynamic, both absorbing and effecting change, all the time, for there will be occasions when all or part of it will be static. A classroom should, however, have the potential, in the way it is set out, what is available in it and how it changes, to support a dynamic exchange with the children. This usually occurs, for example, when a change in the seating arrangements is made or some new object or display is set out. However, a classroom that is

Figure 4.6: Witch Painting

The free flowing and intermixing of the paint is responsible for the quality of this picture. This boy evolved a number of techniques for handling paint in this way.

too fussy or busy, with no quiet spaces to sit or simple things to look at, can be disturbing and cause a child to see nothing. The balance between space and activity, change and familiarity, movement and stillness, is hard to achieve, but the need for it should be recognised. The stimulus and interest arising from what is going on in the classroom will promote language of various kinds. The first exchange will often be through words which will draw attention to, name and share experience. There will also be other forms of sharing and exchange, particularly that of drawing. Gesture and facial expression, form, shape, colour and line, all help children to communicate different aspects of their looking and understanding and especially how they are affected by and respond to what they see and experience. This is especially evident where children are confronted by first-hand experience. To be able to settle down with an object and hold it, to enjoy its qualities is a way of focusing attention on it. Making marks on a piece of paper can heighten observation and probe its qualities leading to a direct visual statement about the experience. There are some experiences and events which cannot be described easily because they involve people doing things, objects moving or being used. In this case it is easier to make a drawing about them than to attempt to encapsulate them in words.

Furthermore, there are many different kinds of drawing media; some are soft and smudgy, some hard and spiky, some waxy and sticky, and yet others are wet and runny. Each one makes possible a choice. Each one has its own way of behaving, allowing certain things to be done well and making others more difficult. It is nice to have a selection of these sometimes and at other times just one or two from which to choose. Such selections and opportunities for choice are ways of extending children's learning.

There is another way in which the experience of being in a classroom can be dynamic and fulfilling, namely through the kinds of things which are brought into it by the teachers, visitors or children. These provide the opportunity of first-hand experience, of a living exchange, with all its uncertainty and strangeness. The tension which can exist when the child is confronted by real things is quite different from that of second-hand experience. An unusual object, plant, stone, animal, piece of machinery, garment or fabric, whatever it is, has its own sensory qualities — its shape and colour and other visual aspects; its size, weight and bulk, its smell or taste, the way it handles and what it feels like to the touch. All these sensations have the potential of nourishing the child's visual memory, ideas and inventiveness and of promoting language, whether words or marks.

First-hand experience of any kind has the quality of sharpening sensory awareness and focusing attention. When this happens to us it is often the case that all kinds of other associations, memories and experiences are evoked. Often these are better expressed and more easily communicated in some visual form rather than by words. In fact, the visual form can itself heighten awareness of the experience and thus enrich the particular experience in the mind and imagination.

In each one of us there will be a rich harvest of associations, some arising from our own family and immediate communities, others from the country's heritage or from religious belief or folk myth. Heroes and heroines, brave men and beasts, epitomising the struggles of good and evil, light and dark which lurk within all of us, find their echo in the stories of a culture.[3] These too can evoke powerful visual images which find their expression in some form of art, and through this the expression of the individual and collective imagination. We know that children will respond to an experience, an environment or an event, as a group, each one finding his own level of involvement and expression yet adding something to the collective experience. Occasions like Hallowe'en or a royal event will show us this. There is also a way in which the group response encourages individuals to make their comment. The making of a model, painting or drawing, can itself rekindle the experience and intensify some of the relationships that were part of it. It is almost as if experience of the real thing enables children to go beyond it into a world of ideas and imagination.

The classroom, as a living, working place, can contain this matrix of influences and stimuli which are continually added to and changed by the work of the children and their teacher to the enrichment of everyone.

To summarise, it is essential to provide young children with the opportunity for a broad sensory experience and not to forget that such experience, at all levels, is essential to the making of art. The natural curiosity of children leads them to elaborate and extend their explorations which enables the perceptive and patient teacher to develop their work in all kinds of ways. The quality and appearance of the classroom are significant in supporting the teacher in this work and particularly in the sensible provision of basic materials and media.

Gradually, as children approach puberty, they become adept at certain skills and make greater demands on themselves and their teachers. It is then that their ideas become of paramount importance.

Notes

1. Daniel Stern, *The First Relationship: Infant and Mother* (Fontana, Opea Books, 1977).

2. Jacob Bronowski, *The Ascent of Man* (BBC Publication, 1976).

3. See Bruno Bettelheim, *The Uses of Enchantment* (Vintage, 1977), pp. 7-11.

5 GETTING TO KNOW THE WORLD

The period of time between self-awareness at seven and self-consciousness at puberty is an important and deceptively 'quiet' one in the growth of children. This is the period when children look at experience more objectively and begin to move out into the world of adults; when they begin to build all kinds of concepts and misconceptions about it; when their own ideas and those of the group are profoundly important. It is a time when children become more socially orientated to the world around them and use adults as models for some of their ideas and undertakings.

How these developments change the way children begin to experience and know the world visually is obviously crucial to work in art education. There are so many sources of visual ideas around in their environment, many of them commercially debased but many exciting and powerful, that children will absorb these influences readily. However, the divorce they experience between them and their own powers of image-making can be frustrating and even distressing.

An important bridge between enriching and extending children's work in art must be an understanding of how children get to know the world and the background from which they do so. Both of these things affect any approach to teaching. All this takes place during the transition between schools in the middle years of childhood.

Getting to know the world at the junior school age can seem to be a matter of growing physically, becoming part of a gang, forming strong friendships, making collections and so on. However, the most significant development, especially for children's art and the way teachers conceive their role in relation to it, is more far-reaching than these.

During the period after the age of seven, children begin to see the world differently because they are able to build concepts about it. This development promotes a number of changes that are important for art education. Physically, they begin to grow, to put on weight, to increase in strength, co-ordination and manipulative range. Physical growth is not uniform: some children may fill out, others put on height, some will become adept at ball skills while others seem to be more clumsy than before.[1]

Such changes affect the way children enjoy physical challenges, whether in sport, play, or working with more demanding and resistant materials. This can also involve increasing the scale and/or intricacy of what is attempted. In physical matters they will begin to look to the world of adults and want to share in, imitate or reflect aspects of the ways in which adults cope physically with their world. This shift in children's capacity to respond physically to the challenges of the world around them can also result in challenges to each other. Identification with their own sex, testing each other out in the group and giving recognition to the 'deeds' and prowess of members of the group are all manifestations of increased physical growth linked with the mental capacity to build concepts, make rules and plan adventures.

Socially the child becomes aware of differences between himself/herself and others. He/she can make comparisons, see similarities and judge differences. Individually or in groups they cherish idols, pop stars, sports heroes and some will soon be making copies from posters or magazines, aping hairstyles and fashions. Children can work at group tasks after this time of change and will allot tasks to each other according to the skills, knowledge or experience which each one is assumed or known to have; one child may be considered best at planning, another at drawing, another good with tools and so on.

This also means that they will learn from each other as much as and often more than they learn directly from the teacher. The range of skills which children can consider important, worth acquiring and will admire will often be inspired by their peer group. Such skills can be very diverse, from blowing bubble gum to drawing hairstyles, shading with pencil or outlining cartoons. Some of these skills may correspond to those which the teacher considers valuable, others will not. Children will be aware of and adopt mannerisms and tricks in art and imitate each other to acquire these. These changes present the teacher with opportunities as well as making difficulties. The opportunities arise from helping children to be more perceptive in looking at and interpreting the images which excite them. Discussion of such images can influence the way children make their own and heighten sensitivity towards the behaviour and forms of different materials.

The difficulties for the teacher are more likely to be in the tolerance of subject matter and patience to help children through gimmicks and methods of working, such as copying, which seem inappropriate or cul-de-sacs which will inhibit personal growth.

Attitudes can be shared, such as 'I'm no good at art' or 'I can't draw', which are as difficult to modify as the positive approval by the children of certain limited kinds of art such as representational stereotypes or cartoon copies. Children, as a group, during this phase can 'adopt' collective responses or attitudes to art or a particular piece of work which are hard to shift by direct confrontation. They may try to satisfy the teacher's expectations in class but have very different views and aspirations away from school. Alternative or 'teacher' opinions may appear to hold sway until a child asks 'Are we doing your art today, Sir, or can we do our own?' or the teacher asks whose art they enjoy most in the group and is surprised by the choice the children make.

This seems to be a time, also, when certain kinds of skill or knowledge which a child may have acquired take on a status quality within the group: 'She's good at horses' or 'He's good at sawing 'cos his Dad showed him'. The teacher should respect this shift in attitude although he will want to find every opportunity to build on children's confidence and to broaden and extend their outlook. Similarly, children will adopt a special material with which they seem to have a particular rapport or knack. Idiosyncratic and sometimes strange ideas and images may also surface strongly at this time, such as the girl who is good at drawing ladies or practised at painting horses or flowers, or the boy interested in trains. Once again the status situation within a group plays a significant part in what children feel they are good at and is worth doing.

All these changes surface as the child grows through the junior, middle and early secondary school years and are closely interrelated with emotional and intellectual changes. Intellectually the ability to build concepts from experience is profoundly significant and creates the foundation for more abstract thought as the individual develops. There is a real ability to plan ahead, to work out strategies, to hold ideas and possibilities together in the mind, whether parts of patterns or notions of wholeness. It is this capacity which enables children at this time to develop the sequences of craft processes and the skills of manipulating tools; to conceptualise problems and sort out ways of resolving them; to draw sides of objects and depict scale and distance; to read drawn patterns and diagrams and plot directions.

One should not doubt that these are real and valuable intellectual skills even though they may be related particularly to direct perception and the manipulation of materials. The way in which the imagination and memory use images and visual ideas to help understand and resolve problems is as important for the developing mind as the way in which they use the symbols and abstractions of words and numbers. Intellectually, the capacity to interpret experience, whether through the kinds of images and forms found in art or the symbols and abstractions found in words and numbers, is a significant and increasingly important way in which meaning is derived from experience. Children explore and invent meanings for themselves through their art. As Bettelheim points out in relation to children's use of fairy stories: 'The child's major problem is to bring some order into the inner chaos of his mind so that he can understand himself better, a necessary preliminary for achieving some congruence between his perceptions and the external world.[2] The search for personal identity and the meaning this gives to many of life's experiences becomes more urgent during puberty. The purpose and point of what is done by an adolescent, or what he or she expects of 'life' is closely related to the way its meaning is interpreted. The making of art as a way of creating one's own order is clearly important in this context; it may be less conscious or conceptual in younger children but nevertheless of great importance. To quote Bettelheim again: 'Sometimes unconscious pressures in children can be worked out through play. But many do not lend themselves to it because they are too complex and contradictory, or too dangerous and socially disapproved.'[2]

Often the particular knowledge or skill which a child may have acquired outside school can be disconcerting to a teacher who has not created the conditions or atmosphere in which such things can be included or discussed. Although children can appear to have some specialised knowledge about certain kinds of images or the skills and practice to achieve particular effects at this time, the way they are understood and how they relate to other forms of knowledge and experience may be lacking. However, it can be damaging for a child not to have the opportunity to communicate and discuss personal knowledge and ideas for he will either feel it is unwanted or of insufficient importance to school learning. What is done at school can then appear to be a different, uninteresting or even alien kind of learning.

The distinction between school-type work and the kind of interests and ideas children want to express in art and through making can often be considerable. A teacher can, therefore, find children's ideas and interests difficult to manage because of his considerably different view of what art is about. Sometimes a lack of expertise or experience will inhibit a teacher from allowing certain ideas to develop but it is more often the problem of accepting and discussing what the child is wanting to do. Yet, it seems to me that this is the most important thing for the teacher to do. Listening to and talking through what children say they want to do, between teacher and child or individual and group, is a significant way of negotiating the aesthetic and practical problems involved. A child can begin to understand the difficulties for himself/herself of finding the right form for his/her ideas and sense the value of thinking through and discussing his/her work rather than expecting it just to work out.

Figure 5.1: Cars

Pages and pages of car drawings like these would not be acceptable to most art teachers as a means to developing visual and aesthetic appreciation. However, this theme — for a while a favourite one — shows the child wrestling with problems of form, viewpoint and three dimensions.

I say this because it is abundantly evident that children's ideas matter considerably to them. In all kinds of circumstances this is so, both from what children say and from the way they behave. It seems from observation that personal ideas have the power to motivate children, to make some task, often self-appointed, seem purposeful or important. Ideas seem to draw on sources of energy in children which seemed otherwise lacking or dormant. I believe this is similar for all of us, for ideas seem to increase motivation or even intensify the energy which goes into some activity whether play or personal learning.

Children's personal and often imaginative ideas about the world as they come to know it range across a wide spectrum of activities. Through ideas they are somehow able to scale down the effect of people, places, events and happenings to manageable proportions and to invent an imaginary world with which they can cope. Some of their ideas can be seen to be wildly wrong, fantastic or over-simplified and yet they still enable children to have confidence to manage their interests, concerns and anxieties — in other words the affairs of living and learning.

In their art and making, the ideas of any group cover a wide spectrum of interests and abilities from purely expressive ones to functional ones. When one observes children playing, this range of activity, from fantasy to technological invention, becomes obvious. It arises in part from a wish to associate with grown up and serious matters and the need for the paraphernalia of play to be suffi-ciently real to sustain the imagination and possible sharing with others.

The need to take the world apart to see how it fits together and works, and then to reassemble it or invent with its parts promotes considerable learning activity at this time. As is suggested in Chap-ter 2, this pattern of behaviour and thinking marks the dawning of the search to make sense of experience and derive personal mean-ing from it. Materials and media perform a profoundly significant role in how the mind develops. Because of its changing capacity to form concepts in concrete, tangible ways, the mind seeks out the kind of experiences with real objects, materials and media on which it can feed. The availability of such experiences is vital to the development of the mind.

Favourite themes to draw and make, programmes on television to watch, teams to support, pop images to idolise are all stimuli to the images which fill the mind. The way in which others behave and think, what they talk about and spend their time doing has a strong effect, by action and reaction, on each individual and has a strong influence on the kinds of things chosen to do in art and thought worthwhile. (See Figure 5.1, p.74.)

It is through these actions, which can be a mixture of fantasy and fact, knowledge and conjecture, that children begin to probe and get to know the world. Although realness becomes important to them as, for example, in drawing, there seems to be another dimension to the images they make which is embedded in their power to excite or interest. The propensity of some children, as they grow towards adolescence, to work from photographs or comics shows this need to relate to such notions as strength, sexuality, aggressiveness or extra-terrestrial phenomena. It seems that art, to be good, has to be real, but real art has to move you. To be moved by cleverness with copying, although it may allure, does not seem to satisfy wholly. There are other worlds to be explored that relate more to what happens inside the individual that the mere representation of real things cannot encompass. The aggressive sexuality of pop music and its associated imagery, the extraordinary power and superhuman events of science fiction become escapes from a more mundane existence and at the same time relate the person to powers within which are at this time latent and difficult to manage. It is here that the core of creative, imaginative endeavour becomes most acutely apparent, where the images created become charged with personal meaning which they cannot fully realise or satisfy.

I believe it is from the moment children are able to build concepts from their experience that this fundamental dilemma of art begins to surface in their work. Simply stated, the problem is one of giving form, through a medium, to their ideas and responses.

At first contact, representing what we see appears to be just a problem of skill or know-how, for, there is the object clearly enough and all we have to do is to set it down in some medium. However, there is much more in the way in which we are selective in our seeing. Memory or association colours and transmutes the images which form in the mind. Once we have the capacity to form concepts, then thoughts, reasons, knowledge, strategies and so on interpose themselves between our response to the object and the way our concept of it is formed by the medium. Copying does not seem to help even though the thing copied can act as a yardstick. It is as though what we see and how we depict it have to find a meeting point. Some aspects of the object are included in the visual image, others are not.

It is as if what we are at any particular time and how we have developed has to find some expression in the forms and images we create and that this is a factor of at least equal importance to our practical skills and knowledge. Although we may work with deliberation, much of what we do will be intuitive and some of it unconscious. This becomes evident in the idiosyncratic character of each individual's art.

'The image is found in the paint, the movement of the paint on the canvas', as Robin Philipson said in a BBC television programme. There is clearly a difference between how a piece of art is conceived and the actual form it takes in practice. This difference is felt as a tension between the content and the medium, between the ideas, emotions, visions and intentions of the individual on the one hand and the experiences, outcomes, shapes and behaviours of the medium — that is visual form — on the other. This content/form tension in creating a piece of art begins to be felt as the capacity to build concepts develops, and it is noticeable in the things children say.[3]

Children will say that things look wrong, the paint won't mix, they can't draw and so on, all revealing the tension between what they visualise and what emerges through the medium; thus the period of development from seven onwards is extremely important in the growth of the individual's sensitivity to images and the way these can arise and be given form.

The content/form tension is really only resolved in the kind and quality of image that is produced. Children learn to read images of all kinds without necessarily discriminating between them. It is when they become more serious and discerning about their own image-making that they can focus on the particular way in which images are constructed. The ability to 'read' sophisticated images is clearly something which children can learn to do with considerable personal enrichment as the Schools Council Project 'Critical Studies in Art Education' has shown.

Gary, a second-year junior, wrote after visiting an exhibition of sculptures.

My drawing of the sow is coloured white and brown. The sculpture of the sow is made of rosewood and marble, it had fine grains. It feels smooth when your fingers stroke its back and your fingers go into the grains. It was carved by Ted Roocroft. He used a mallet, chisel, V tool and gouge.[4]

In talking with artists and craftsmen about their work, children's perceptions are heightened and their range of visual ideas extended. Getting to know the world should, therefore, include responding to images and finding the source and nourishment for image-making in their own looking. Here, teachers have an important part to play.

Of course, superficial images of one sort or another can be made in all kinds of ways which have little meaning beyond the processes and techniques which produce them. Quality of observation, sensitivity to materials and power of imagination need not be called upon in order to follow a process mechanically, for such personal elements are far more hazardous and unpredictable in the production of a work of art. It is these elements which lead the individual forward into new realms of personal experience which the following of a technical process can seldom do.

For example, some form of print making will create print-type images which can be used as a justification for the work done, regardless of whether they have engaged the child in the content/ form tension which is the source of real understanding in art. Children can soon feel that a process (such as producing a print) is pointless if they just go on producing work mechanically with little real focusing on the print qualities and discussion of the kind of visual effects which can be achieved.

Producing lots of prints can keep children busy and the apparent ease of some of the processes can be very seductive. However, the particular possibilities for producing printed images linked with an awareness of the pervasive manner in which they are used in our culture are important ways through which children can become more observant and discriminating.

Throw-away and scrap materials of all kinds are a popular source of material for art sessions in primary schools. If they are used without considerable care, such materials produce waste and scrap-type images in which the shapes and forms of the found material over predict what can be done and the bizarre effects they produce can become a justification for the art children produce.

If these materials are offered it is absolutely necessary, in my view, to help children to explore, take apart, play around and experiment with such materials before they attempt to organise them into visual forms. It may also be necessary, for the teacher to classify and present such materials in particular ways. For example, waste materials could be presented according to the substance from which they are made or the shapes they have. Waste and found materials can help children to see that in making art they are not concerned with imitation of nature or the exact copying of things seen, but in re-ordering, inventing and interpreting what they see and imagine in another form. In this way any material becomes an artistic medium as Eisner suggests.[5]

Here the teacher can both help children and subvert their deeper concerns. To help children is to lead them to understand the forms and images of art. To hinder them is to replace this search with fatuous, time-consuming processes, which the teacher might understand and approve but which children find as empty as the mechanical pursuit of any process whose point is lost in the mere production of artefacts. For example, some form of print making will create print-type images, the production of which can keep children busy with the process and be seductive because of the apparent ease of production. Busyness and production can be used as a justification for the activity. However, the content/form tension which is produced most readily by working from the real world can be subverted by the technical processes involved and the ease of obtaining results. Thus, it is possible to find teachers using forms of art with children which side-step the deeper need to wrestle with realness and image reality. Such forms seem to be art made from art-making methods rather than art which grows from real seeing and personal encounters. The dividing line between these two experiences is fine but results from a profoundly different understanding of art and belief in the capacity of young people to make personal statements through it. Perhaps an over-emphasis on certain kinds of result, irrespective of the personality, aptitudes and ideas of children or the qualities and demands of particular materials, is a mark of the art-making approach.

Of course there are all kinds of personal encounters which stimulate the need to respond through an art medium rather than in other ways. Perhaps it is the way in which the outcomes register personal ideas and ways of seeing or feeling which best enable the teacher to relate to them as images. Apparent distortions of shape, idiosyncracies of colour, over-simplification of form, exaggerations of scale or relationship are not just 'mistakes' or 'incompetence'. There is always the possibility that such elements in a child's work show the beginnings of a capacity to form personal statements arising from a genuine response and visual perceptiveness. However, the most appropriate means of communicating ideas and visions are not self-evident to children. There is a lot of hard work, searching about and disappointment in the act of finding and making the images which are most appropriate to the experience. Herein lies the most profound aspect of the teacher's task when supporting children in their creative endeavours.

The ways in which a teacher helps young people to know the world through the validity of their own interpretations is a key issue at this stage of their development.

In this, the notion of interpretation has to be taken seriously and seen as being richer in content and function than copying (whether a cartoon or a plant), description (whether a Roman soldier or biological specimen) or representation (whether the copy of a photograph or a shell). The teacher himself must be seen to interpret the work children do by the manner in which he discusses it. It seems to me that it is not sufficient just to accept what a child does nor yet to dismiss it. There has to be a correspondence of some kind between the child, his work and the teacher; between the qualities apparent in the work, what the child can say about it and the observations and understanding of the teacher. When the teacher manages to bring these aspects into relationship then I believe that positive learning takes place.

Any teacher, whether trained in art or not, can do this because two of the main skills are looking carefully and listening. For example, consider the qualities of the materials used and how the child may have brought these out in his/her work, irrespective of the exactness of the drawing. Furthermore, what has the child noticed? Is there evidence of this in the work, however slight, or can the child, perhaps, only talk about it?

In any case, the more a teacher attempts to evolve approaches to looking at children's work with them, the easier it becomes. It will then be realised that the processes involved in making a piece of art are closely associated with ways of getting to know the world, which are very different from and sometimes complementary to talking and writing about it.

Part of this approach may include relating a child's work to pieces of work by other children or to work by artists from different periods and cultures. Such activity gives any work produced — and the understandings which might arise because of it — a wider

Figure 5.2: Log of Wood

This drawing shows an aspect of interpretation where the response to some quality in the object, whether visual, tactile or spatial, affects considerably the form of the drawing and the way in which the medium is handled.

aesthetic and visual context which is both educationally more sound than a teacher opinion and able to increase confidence in child and teacher to look at and talk about art.

Of course, such an approach to sharing children's art is concerned with interpretation (the different ways in which people see things and handle images) and not with copy, representation or description.

In copying, the object of the copy dominates almost exclusively, intentionally or unconsciously, the visual appearance or image produced. In making a description or representation, the thing observed or the referent commands attention to the exclusion of more personal or imaginative responses. In making an interpretation, the effect of the object on the person, the individual way in which he or she responds and the way that response is coloured by memory and association dominate — more or less — the visual encounter and its outcome. This experience is not wholly satisfying until the techniques and means of managing the material and visual language approximate to the idea or image evoked in the mind. Thus, the notion of interpretation is so much richer than that of representation or copy. (See Figure 5.2, p.81.)

The confidence to discuss children's work at all, let alone in an interpretive way, takes time to achieve, yet it is the single most important educational experience in which to engage children in my view, and the most positive way out of stating purely subjective preferences. Furthermore, I believe it could be the way to raise levels of intelligence concerning visual and aesthetic experience, neither of which can logically develop independently from the experience of looking at and responding to art, and, in terms of children being educated, actually making art. The act of making images and forms enables the individual to get inside the experience with all its frustrations, uncertainties, satisfactions, disappointments, achievements and so forth. I believe the experience of actually handling materials to be different in kind and quality from just looking at the results and neither one should supplant the other in the art education of children.

Therefore the kinds of discussion and looking which arise from interpretation have the potential to engage the children and the teacher with the central dilemma of making art, namely that of ideas, visions and purposes finding form and expression in a medium: the content/form tension. The teacher has to help children to become more aware of, or more intelligent about, this dilemma, and notions of interpretation are able to do this. Visual and aesthetic intelligence develops through such things as careful observation of the qualities of media and the particular ways in which they are used; of appearances and relationships and how these are changed or developed in art from different cultures and periods of time; of the effects and influence of different kinds of stimuli and materials on the forms produced. Approaches to sharing and discussing such things arise through a willingness to do so and belief in its value educationally. One of the outcomes is an openness to different ways of seeing and a capacity and confidence to discuss and share experience.

Getting to know the world at this age, when the child is developing between the dawn of self-awareness around the age of seven and puberty somewhere after eleven or twelve, is very much to do with the selections he and his peer group make for understanding it. The availability of different kinds of contact and stimuli in the environment also determine how children come to know the world.

But what of the developments of personal imagery at this time? Apart from certain skills, children also develop particular interests and knowledge depending on the opportunities open to them. For example, using tools or sewing materials, enjoying make-up or dress, developing sports and pastimes, being caught up in work or petty crime and so on. Each new set of relationships can bring with it significant ways of seeing oneself and interpreting images and finding an identity in the widening horizons of the adult world.

Any of the above developments can be the means for personal satisfaction and growth (even if this is reduced to the capacity to survive) and create opportunities to make relationships with others. Yet, it is difficult for these life experiences to find some form of expression through art. Drawings and paintings are usually expected to satisfy the criteria of exact detail, correct proportion and realism in shape or outline. Such criteria will often be recognised by the whole group as 'good art' but, at the same time, can inhibit a different or extended exploration of personal ideas and ways of looking.

Even so, outside the expectations and demands of the classroom or the secondary school art studio, children will often gather round them the pictures and objects which excite and interest them although they may lack the confidence and means to create their own visual statements. In looking at many exhibitions of art work for examinations in secondary schools, I have been struck by the obvious differences, sometimes glaring, between the kind of images a child has worked with at home and those which they are encouraged or expected to produce in the school art studio. The difference between these two sources of art work seems to be that of learning about visual matters which exist in one's environment and making art. I believe, however, that it is slightly but importantly different from this, and that it involves discussing ways of looking and perceiving before the means of making images are assumed. In other words, the necessity of making interpretations needs to be understood before the assumptions about making art dominate.

To cite a particularly clear example, I recall seeing the flower drawings and paintings by a boy whose work was on show for moderation in an examination. Clearly he had produced a number of flower pieces at home and had become adept at doing so. Yet they showed a weakness in drawing arising from poor observation, so that the formulae he had adopted left little scope for visual development since the source of ideas for doing so was restricted to representational formulae. However, there was also evidence of the teacher having him experiment with abstraction in shape and colour, unrelated to plant forms.

The point at issue seemed to be not that he needed to make some proper art which demonstrated awareness of visual qualities of shape, colour and so on, but that he needed to look at and develop his understanding and awareness of the visual qualities of

Figure 5.3: World with Force Field

The motivation to handle the visual problems of form and space is stronger because of the chosen subject matter.

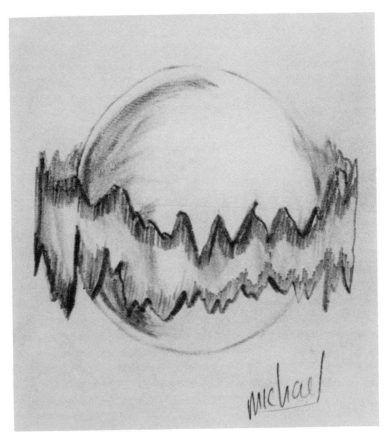

the plants he was drawing. In this way, the means of interpreting the experience of plants could have led to a more appropriate and imaginative use of visual language. The things he could have found out about transparency, brilliance, juxtaposition and forms of colour would have enabled him to translate his experience of plants into the language of visual form. He would thereby be able to develop his capacity to relate this form to those found elsewhere than in his own art. While his personal endeavours remain locked into representational clichés and his studio work divorced from his reality in abstract concepts, this would be unlikely to happen.

Because children find it difficult to work with the visual ideas and images of art it does not mean, in my view, that they do not want to do so. It is that such norms as exactness and detail act as inhibitors in their confidence to explore visual ideas in a practical way. Where they do show evidence of this interest in visual ideas is in the collections of pictures displayed in bedrooms or collected from magazines — in forms of dress and make-up and their attraction to visual aspects of pop culture. Sometimes they will copy these and through the process of copying learn ways of drawing and representing which will be used in their own image-making.

It is during this period of development that children can evolve a visual eclecticism through which they accumulate particular selections of visual ideas from such sources as fashion or pop magazines and the world of science fiction. Children will borrow, copy and adapt visual ideas and symbols from any source to include in and extend their own image-making. Thus, in their art, it is possible to see a wide range of image ideas culled from different sources, some borrowed from friends, others lifted from magazines and others relying on simple, perhaps more childlike, schemata. Even so, amongst all these there will be images arising from deep interest and genuine observation as well as from sensitive teaching and perceptive criticism. (See Figure 5.3, p.84.)

The peer groups can regulate, sustain or intensify these ways of finding and using image ideas. One child may copy or imitate another; others will take up a particular visual idea or symbol and use it in their own way. Themes, techniques, approaches and ideas are exchanged and assimilated into their visual approaches and vocabularies just as they are in their verbal language and dress. These are all ways through which children get to know the world and grow towards adolescence.

A child who has been shown some visual trick or way of hand-

Figure 5.4: Girls with a Mirror
Getting to know the world is very much a matter of coming to terms with oneself especially as one approaches puberty.

ling a medium by an older brother or friend may feel that this is especially valuable and want to share it with his friends, where it can soon become part of the visual vocabulary of the group.

All these developments accompany a changed relationship to adults whose various roles are becoming more clearly differentiated in the mind of the child. They will become more adept at reading expressions, understanding implications, learning mannerisms and knowing what is valued and what rejected. Children will also be maturing sexually and be aware of the processes of change in themselves. Clothes, fashions, facial and general physical appearances will all matter. Grouping and pairing will heighten this development and intensify awareness of self. It is beyond the scope of this book to discuss further the way in which this relates to art education and the work of teaching, but it seems important to mention this aspect of maturation so that the developments throughout this age range are placed in context. The dawning of sexual maturity and all that this means is clearly significant in the way in which children get to know the world and derive personal meaning from it. (See Figure 5.4, p.86.)

To summarise: the capacity to build concepts from experience is a profound and far-reaching change which permeates much of what children do in art after the age of seven. If a teacher is to understand how best to extend and enrich children's experience of art at this time, he/she must be aware of the different way children are getting to know the world. A teacher must become aware and informed of the changes which follow from children's capacity to build concepts and not least how this development initiates the tension between the content and form of their art.

The challenge for the teacher is to find ways to help children to develop their powers of observation and critical awareness through which this distinction between copying and interpreting, representing and inventing can be discussed and understood. These developments form an important preparation for adolescence.

Notes

1. See J.C. Pearce, *Magical Child* (Paladin, 1979), p.151.
2. Bruno Bettelheim, *The Uses of Enchantment* (Vintage, 1977), p. 53.
3. See Jerome Bruner, *On Knowing* (The Belknap Press, Harvard University, 1980), pp. 62-3.
4. See R. Taylor, *The Illuminating Experience* (Schools Council Critical Studies in Art Education, 1982).
5. Elliott Eisner, *Educating Artistic Vision* (Collier Macmillan, 1972), p. 81.

6 TEACHING ART

Each one of us responds differently to experience; we have different memories and associations; we develop different patterns of understanding and belief and we see and feel differently. In the field of art education, the uniqueness of each person's experience and how this may be reflected in his/her art is especially valued. However, the standpoint of unique individuality can be in conflict with the role and purpose of the teacher whose educational aims may not always be able to accommodate such variety and difference as this suggests.

This chapter examines the relationship between the teacher's intention and the child's response and suggests how these might be related. Technical knowledge and practical skill are discussed and put into context with the development of perception and personal ideas.

Therefore, the ideas presented here are central to the argument about how the teacher extends and focuses children's education in art without denying them their individuality. The problems this poses for teaching are considered in the light of a particular model of relationships which forms the basis for the argument in the following chapter.

In one Victorian school I knew, which must have been a very prestigious building when it was first put up in 1880, there were the visible remains of the tiered seating in several classrooms. These remnants of an educational environment governed by school boards also tell us that such a building exemplified a certain approach and underlying attitude towards schooling. The teacher stood at the front of the class, either on a dais or behind a desk, with the forty or more scholars sitting before him. Embedded in this approach to teaching was the central belief that schooling is to do with the acquisition of knowledge imparted by the teacher.

Teachers and their books were the repositories of knowledge from which children had to learn. Whatever way the teacher divided, sorted, classified and presented his material, the proof of success was how well his pupils could recite it back to him. This approach to education was knowledge-based and the concern of the teacher was to 'package' items of knowledge in such a way that children of different ages could grasp them. The teacher would judge the results in terms of his/her own estimation of what was worth knowing. Diagrammatically this approach can be seen to be linear; that is, the work of the children would be contained within the teacher's perception of what knowledge and supporting skills had to be acquired.

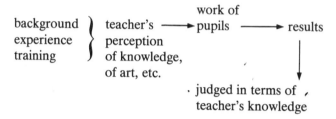

The manner in which the child's learned knowledge had to be demonstrated related directly to the teacher's perceptions of knowledge and did not account for any of the child's idiosyncrasies; furthermore, little account was taken of the child's own discoveries, interests and responses.

Obviously the teacher's perception of knowledge and what could or should be grasped by his pupils affected the actual work done and the way in which it was judged. This approach was evident in art as much as any area of the curriculum. Examples would be drawn on the chalkboard to be copied by the pupils and the result closest to that of the teacher would be considered the best. Even when objects were provided as models for drawing or painting the manner in which the work was conceived and presented was clearly set out by the teacher; the way of looking at the object and the way of setting down what was seen were largely imposed by the teacher.

I remember hearing Robin Tanner,[1] whose work in the field of art education has been so outstanding, describe an experience which he had as a schoolchild.

> On a sleepy autumn afternoon in 1910, when I was six, I brought at my teacher's request, sprays of bluish-mauve Michaelmas Daisies for brushwork. I arrived early, and she told me to strip the flowers and place a sprig for every child. This

seemed a pity to me: the tall branched sprays were so handsome, and the little oddments I laid along the desks had wilted by the time the registers had been called. Moreover, our teacher made no reference to them at all. It was a nice feeling squeezing out dabs of Sap Green — the colour of evil pond water — and blue — the colour of cold hands — into china dishes and placing a brush beside each as for a meal. Our teacher gave out sheets of paper of intimidating whiteness and we began to paint. She pinned hers to the blackboard and demonstrated each step. First we were caused to paint a Sap Green stalk down the middle of the page, with leaves of single blobs on either side. Then with the sickly Blue our teacher showed how to arrange petal-blobs to form the flower: the first to the North, then one to the South, now one to the East and one to the West, and now the tiresome job of squeezing four more into N.W., S.W., S.E., and N.E., and lo! there was our Michaelmas Daisy. Sadly, we disregarded its mounded golden centre with the curled pistils and bright stamens I loved so much.

There was such an acreage of paper still untouched that without a thought I painted another daisy, and another, and another, and a whole fat bunch of them. I painted a Sap Green vase for them, which I decorated with bands of Blue. I stood my vase in a window, and painted draped curtains, spotted blue and tied with blue bows. And coming down the garden path beyond I painted a green-habited postman bearing a blue letter in his hand. I was flushed with excitement. A frame seemed right for my picture, so I used the remains of my own and my neighbour's ration to paint one. It was splendid. I didn't know where I was: I had lost my teacher and the classroom and forgotten all my monitorial duties ... — Until H.M. Inspector, who was visiting the school that day, came into the classroom! Our teacher ordered us to hold up our work for him to admire, saying she was sure that mine would be the best. 'But whatever has happened?' she asked in astonishment. 'Bring it for me to see,' and I bore my precious picture as though I was bearing a masterpiece.

I only remember my tears and the note 'Governess' gave me to take to my parents after I had stood in the corner of the room with my face to the wall until the end of the day. But I loved that Inspector, who told me I had been rather naughty but it was 'a capital picture'.

Robin's piece of work did not follow the expected pattern and contradicted the teacher's perception of a 'correct' flower painting. In fact, the child's painting went beyond the teacher's knowledge of how to do it because his response to the plant and the paint was deeper and more personal. Unfortunately for Robin, it was not the teacher's scheme of things to accept his ideas and responses as part of the work.

The ideas of Marion Richardson, another influential educationist in the field of art, showed us that the imagination and response of the child was to be valued, perhaps prized, above all else: '. . . the growing respect for the individuality of the child. In art this respect is a necessity, for unless a child is expressing his own vision he is expressing nothing at all.'[2]

The spontaneous release which became the hallmark of child art led teachers to expect something quite different from their teaching than a stereotyped, simplified adult image. The simple, naïve paintings, rhythmic and colourful in appearance, seemed to accord much more with the observed nature of the young child. Such paintings were certainly produced with more zest and involvement and revealed the special way in which children saw and responded to the world around them, and enjoyed sensuously the qualities of materials like paint.

This shift in approach meant that the teacher's perceptions of the task set had to take into account the response of the child. Such a response could very considerably from child to child. Some would be motivated by the teacher's stimulus and want to start work immediately; others, feeling confused, would be unable to find a starting point from the stimulus and play with the material or follow another child's lead. Despite the problem of the unpredictability of a child's response, once the step of taking it into consideration had been made, it was impossible to consider the effectiveness of teaching without it. Therefore, the simple way of judging the child's learning by direct correspondence to the teacher's teaching became considerably more difficult.

This situation was especially evident in art teaching where the unique, individual mark became valued as the trace of personal involvement and individual learning. However, taking into account individual responses did, and still does, create problems when assessing the worth of what resulted. No longer could the teacher rely on his perception of what the result should look like; no longer could a blackboard example guide and predict the results or be used as a yardstick against which to assess them. Everything, it seemed, had changed and become more unpredictable and less amenable to general standards. The demonstration to be followed and the stereotype as a standard measurement no longer helped the teacher to judge the worth of what children produced in their art.

Nevertheless, having said this, I realise that many teachers in primary schools do rely heavily on suggestions, examples and approaches found in popular art and craft magazines, on television, and on other sources as both a starting point and, by inference, a yardstick for children's art. Perhaps teachers who rely on these sources for the art education they promote with children do not realise how much such sources can predict the work children do and what kind of standards are implied by using them.[3] In many ways there is a parallel between this attitude to art teaching and that of teachers in 1910, there being little difference, in effect, between providing a 'how to do it' from a magazine or television and drawing an example to be followed on a chalkboard. The subject matter, materials and content may have changed but not the underlying attitude which assumes that children produce satisfactory art by following instructions or models.

This is not to disparage the difficulties many teachers find in teaching art nor the effort they put into seeking a solution to these difficulties. The reason I draw attention to the demonstration, example directed approach to art teaching is to look at the problem of teaching art in a different way. Whatever approach is used, however many different ways of getting children to do things, the problem of how to include the child's responses and ideas, in work which the teacher feels is appropriate and worthwhile, has to be faced.

Of course, anyone who lacks confidence or know-how, but has to teach art for at least part of the week, will find ways round this problem. These may include such approaches as providing new materials, techniques or 'ideas' for each and every session. Or, a stock of well tried and proven topics which seem to have a seasonal or festive justification may be tried. However, whatever ways are devised for giving children art to do, the basic problem still exists of how to include the personal responses of the child yet retain the sense of direction and purpose of the teacher.

What becomes apparent, as soon as one attempts to include children's responses, is that the linear pattern of learning breaks down and there is difficulty in the teacher's maintaining the narrow direction of the work as it was conceived. This seems to be true whether one is following some personal notion of what the children should do or following a magazine or television recipe. The children's responses will shift the direction of the teacher's objectives.

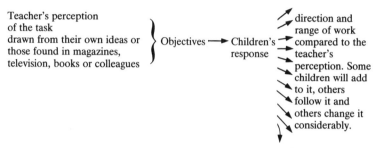

Teacher's perception of the task drawn from their own ideas or those found in magazines, television, books or colleagues } Objectives → Children's response → direction and range of work compared to the teacher's perception. Some children will add to it, others follow it and others change it considerably.

Often, the way in which a child sees and understands something is very different from that of the teacher, however carefully approached by the latter. Even the efforts to please the teacher can contradict his objectives and the intention of the teacher is not realised in the work he hoped the children would do. It seems, therefore, that the teacher has to take account of children's responses rather than circumvent or control them. In any case, is it ever possible to control the response in another if this response is manifestly imaginative, personal and creative? In fact, many teachers will conceive and plan their work in art in relation to the likely responses of the children they anticipate teaching.

Yet, control, in an overt and direct manner, is one of the ways most frequently adopted by teachers in order to cope with having to do art with children. For example, cutting out or drawing the shapes to be coloured or pre-mixing paints are examples of teachers controlling what children do. Various reasons will be stated for this kind of teacher control, such as the mess children will get into when handling material in their own way or their lack of technical knowledge. It is often assumed that the child's inability to perform in ways the teacher expects is because the child has not sufficient technical knowledge or practical skill to do so. Thus, in this instance, it could seem that the task of the teacher is one of teaching a technique and demonstrating particular ways of working. He may even feel that some practice of a skill for its own sake is necessary.

This assumption, that children lack technical knowledge or practical skill, seems to have more validity in the junior school than the infant school, as children of this age are beginning to doubt their own creative ability and seek satisfaction from skills alone. These skills may be in handling a tool or material or in copying found images. Yet, the assumption that a child has little skill or know-how may only be valid within the context of the teacher's set task. In some areas children of junior school age can develop sophisticated skills but in a narrow range. The more closely the teacher's task is defined the less scope there is for a child to solve the problems posed in his own way, thus exaggerating the child's apparent lack of skill. Yet, children can be very inventive when the circumstances and their personal confidence are right and in this way develop skills appropriate to the task in hand.

The key seems to be to find appropriate levels of technical knowledge which match relevant and personal levels of skill. Of course there are occasions when a child will be frustrated by a lack of technique which no amount of skill will make up for, or the level of skill in relation to the task will not be sufficient to avoid disappointment and frustration. For example, a child may have certain skills in handling paint yet not have considered possible ways of creating textured surfaces. Simple technical help, in these circumstances, could initiate a whole range of new developments.

The problem seems to require an understanding of the relationship between the teaching of technique and the development of skill, for techniques can be taught in any number of ways but will always remain conceptual and outside the real understanding of the individual until they are practised as a skill. Furthermore, it is vital to understand such a relationship in order to perceive the right time and manner of intervention in the development of a child's work.

One reason why the teaching of technique is often used as the main input by the teacher is that the teacher's objectives can be reaffirmed through it. The direction and purpose of the work can be maintained towards results he can understand and justify. Techniques can also be shown which minimise the degree of skill which children have to use. For example, the production of painted textures can be arranged so that however inadequate children's pictures might be, textured surfaces will be in evidence. The use of sponge techniques for skies, stiff brushes for grass, splatter and crumpled paper work can all produce paint textures with the minimum of skill and even less creative imagination. In some cases I have seen the teacher doing all the hard bits for the children, such as cutting out the shape for the children to colour or providing templates for them to draw round. Teaching technique also seems to be something tangible and positive which the teacher can do to improve children's art. To actually show how something should be done seems to make the problem of what is worth doing, and what the child wants to express, less pressing. At least the teacher has done some teaching even if many of the children do not understand it and, even more, cannot see its relevance!

Individuality and Art Education

Having written this, it will soon be necessary for me to say something about the relationship between technique and skill, but before I do so it is important to look at another approach to dealing with the major problem of including children's own responses in the work the teacher wants them to do — namely, citing individual development as the purpose of art education, the teacher can rationalise the diversity of results, few of which accord with his intention, by saying that it is individuality which counts and that is what the teacher is really seeing in any range of work. Thus the teacher may never need to meet the problem of children's art work contradicting his intention because the intention is to reveal and foster individuality. This contention can be cited as a reason for not teaching technique as children will find technique out for themselves and would have their individuality inhibited by the direct teaching of this. Further, it could be asserted that it is the differences between individuals which give their art its greatest validity and such differences cannot be assessed in terms of generalised standards which the direct teaching of technique may produce. Thus the use of templates which produce exactly the same image is unpardonable as is any form of overt control or direction of what children do in art. Why bother to be a teacher, one may ask, if one is only caretaking individuality? Individuality, as a major premise on which the aims of art teaching are built, cannot be valid, for it is not just art that is concerned with fostering individuality. To place the emphasis of art teaching on the growth of the individual is to suggest that the subject, the realm of meaning and human endeavour we label Art, is of little actual consequence.

For the individual to grow in sensitivity and awareness to art and visual ideas and images his individuality in this respect must grow because of art, not as a vague denial of it. As Eisner suggests, many things which are claimed for art education can be claimed for a host of other fields as well. He states 'The prime value of the arts in education lies in the unique contributions it makes to the individual's experience with and understanding of the world.'[3]

Overstating the cause of individuality as the aim of art education leads to purely idiosyncratic and subjective arguments being used when it comes to appreciating and assessing what is done, and the teacher's exchanges with children will remain on a subjective level of personal preference. How is the child going to achieve any intelligence about visual matters if this is so? Presumably teaching art must be about art as much as individuality even though the outcomes may be highly individual.

It is perhaps important to state this another way: the growth of the individual must be the concern of every educator and the more we understand about that growth, the more we will be able to provide for it. However, such growth should not be interpreted and committed narrowly, in terms of intellectual or vocational development alone. A capacity to respond to experience in different ways, an awareness of the need to grow in imagination and sensitivity, an ability to visualise and use one's visual memory, to design and invent, are all aspects of growth we should cherish. None of these things is an independent entity but is part of that broad intelligence that enables us to live more fully.

Art is profoundly important for the full growth of the individual because it deals with ideas, feelings and experiences visually and develops a language of visual, tactile and spatial responses which create and sustain images. To develop an intelligence about visual matters is not a haphazard affair any more than it is with other languages. Experiences of looking, and interpreting, analysing and solving problems, visualising and finding appropriate forms and images for our feelings and ideas are all capable of refinement and enrichment through teaching.

That art deals with visual ideas and develops a language of responses, that it creates and sustains images is profoundly important for the growth of the individual in particular ways. It is individual growth which arises because of the capacity to develop and respond to visual and aesthetic experiences that is significant and the fact that art is the means whereby this happens.

It is the individual's growth in response to visual and aesthetic ideas, his own use of them and his capacity to use and respond to images — his own and others — that is peculiar to art education, not his growth *per se*. If we are teaching art, we must believe that there is something inherent in art that is worth teaching. To raise the level of intelligence in children in these matters must be a prime concern of art education and should not be passed off as being capable of subjective interpretation only. It is through understanding art education in this way that the basis for art teaching will be stated.

Experience or Results

Another way of avoiding the contradiction between the teacher's intention and the child's response is to say that it is the journey that counts, not the arrival; the experience, not the result. Clearly the two are closely related, for however we may deny the importance of results, many children are affected by them. There is as much positive feedback from results as from experience, though the two are different. The experience of making art is a continually fluctuating one, in which small achievements and discoveries are countered by difficulties and frustrations. This is especially so after we develop self-awareness when concepts about how things ought to look vie with more direct and spontaneous responses. When knowing about, and responding to, become separate experiences, the difference between the activity of doing and the fixity of completing become far more apparent.

Yet, it is the tension between the response and the form which the medium takes; between the ideas and their resolution; between the content of a piece and its form, which lies at the very heart of creative endeavour: the content/form tension which has been described in Chapter 5. It is, therefore, very misleading and ultimately damaging to suggest or behave as though the two had nothing to do with each other. The importance of this relationship will be brought out again later and suggestions offered as to how it might become central to the development of children's understanding of art.

The result is never quite an end and is as much a confirmation of what is known and understood at any particular time as it is a final or absolute entity. A result exists as tangible evidence of the happening or series of experiences which produced it. Until it is destroyed it can be referred to and become a part of that individual's recorded history; he can be known by it whether he himself is known or not.

To dismiss the result in preference to the experience is as educationally unsound as to ignore the experience as being an essential part of the result. The two things are closely related and should be understood in that light. Thus, it seems necessary to understand something of the process involved in the making as well as developing a capacity to discuss and 'read' results. This is one reason why it is valuable for teachers to take part in practical in-service courses where they can get on the inside of the process; where they can experience the frustration of not having the right technique yet having to acquire it at the right time; or achieve the satisfaction of finding a result which they had not been able to conceive outside the experience of handling media. It seems to me that an awareness of the continually fluctuating interdependence of completed statements and exploratory searching while forming art media into objects and images is indispensible to teaching.

Getting inside the process of using media also enables the teacher to see the relationship between the perceptions and ideas which are stimulated and the responses which focus the activity of doing. It becomes evident that if a child's responses seem to misread or wrongly interpret the teacher's perception of a task, then the reverse is true, for a teacher's response can misread the way a child sees something. I have often been aware that my response to a child's perception has lacked understanding or observation. We may show a child something which has particular interest for us only to find that his response is out of phase. It may not be lack of stimulation or disinterest on the part of the child, that causes this so much as a different focus of attention or a different centre of response. I remember looking at an old house with my son when he was eight years old and trying to discuss the shapes and materials from which it was made. He seemed disinterested until he suddenly remarked on the pattern of the chimneys! The kind of preparation which the teacher makes, and the discussion which takes place between him and the child enable these differences to be resolved in a positive and fruitful way. An insistence by the teacher on the child's understanding his perception can increase the conflict or apathy in the child. Teachers and children should learn how to share and negotiate their particular ways of seeing, interests and points of view, especially where these touch on meaning.

Despite the most clever teaching of technique, the problem remains of children using their own level of skill to interpret technique and use it in their own way to develop understanding. For a technique means nothing until it is mastered, at whatever level, as a personal skill. It can thus be seen that children need to acquire levels of appropriate skill if the art they produce is to progress with confidence. However, if what they do is to retain its meaning for them, a level of technical accomplishment and practised skill is not enough to sustain them. Ultimately, the extension of their perceptions into ever widening experiences and the enrichment of their responses is necessary to give their art its meaning.

Here I am deliberately suggesting that perception and response, technique and skill are intimately and crucially linked when an individual is working creatively with media and this linking can be observed. It is this crucial linking that makes the intervention of the teacher in the creative work of children so difficult. Therefore I propose to set these relationships out as a working model which I can use to discuss the way in which teachers relate to children making art. This model sets out the relationships between these four areas in a dynamic rather than linear way as this seems, from observation and personal practice, a useful way to examine more closely the work of the art teacher.

To recap, *the linear model* shows how teachers work when they teach from a knowledge base which anticipates a specific kind of result.

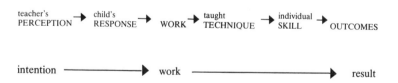

teacher's PERCEPTION → child's RESPONSE → WORK → taught TECHNIQUE → individual SKILL → OUTCOMES

intention ————→ work ————————→ result

The dynamic model, on the other hand, is used to describe the way children learn in art when their responses are taken into consideration and the interaction of the teacher therefore becomes more difficult.

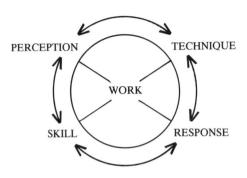

This diagram will be used to discuss the role of the teacher when interacting with the responses of children. First, however, some definitions will be given for each of the terms used.

Perception: (a) the thing perceived — whether an object, phenomenon or the behaviour and hoped-for outcome of some piece of work by a child; (b) the sensory awareness of something; the focusing of attention which enables a sharpness or clarity in one's senses or a sense; the understanding of things experienced and the penetration of them by individual or group states of awareness; critical awareness.

Response: reaction — manner of being affected by actual experience; change in emotions and feelings in association with memory and imagination, the altering or modifying of behaviour by stimulation — bringing into focus existing ideas and concepts so that they relate to or combine with new experience in personal and imaginative ways.

Technique: method, approach, pattern of handling tools, materials or processes — often evolved through practice and experience and handed down through tradition and teaching; kinds of knowledge about art and ways of creating visual appearances.

Skill: facility, expertise; ability to apply and adapt techniques to personal ends; skill develops through motivation and the practised involvement with materials and media; skill is not seen as mere co-ordination but the capacity to visualise and handle visual, plastic and spatial ideas.

It is interesting to compare these four areas with Eisner's four general factors that appear related to the production of visual art forms.[4]

Having now made some attempt to define terms it is necessary to say why these terms should be arranged in a circle as they are. The reason for this is to indicate the dynamic relationship between these terms, in which no one has precedence or sequence over the others. For example, discovering or being shown a technique can generate considerable response, or it can promote the need to play with the medium to acquire a level of skill, or it can heighten perception about some aspect of one's experience. In fact, it would be possible to enter into the work of making a piece of art by starting at any of these four terms because each term is an inseparable form of experience necessary to making art. Some practical examples will, I hope, make these ideas clearer.

Heightening a child's perception may promote a response where the child wants to set to work immediately and seems full of ideas about what to do. However, ideas have to find some kind of form in media and once the child attempts to work with media a number of other things can happen. Firstly, the original perception, arising from the teacher's stimulus, can begin to fade as it fails to be realised in the form the media takes. On the other hand, the ideas and skill at producing them may be sufficient but the knowledge of technique to enable the child to overcome certain basic problems is lacking.

As the work develops and ideas become, say, more complex or sophisticated, the level of skill with which the medium is handled is inadequate to realise the ideas. Lastly, despite the teacher's stimulus and/or the teaching of a technique, the child seems to lack any personal response and few ideas seem to be forthcoming.

It is possible to distinguish four conditions which stop the work of children from progressing and require the help and interaction of the teacher in some form or another: (1) the perception fades, (2) knowledge or technique may be lacking, (3) the level of skill is inadequate to the task in hand and (4) the response is lacking and they have few ideas. Let us consider each of these in turn.

(1) The Perception Fades

Anyone whose perceptions have been stimulated to communicate something through a medium will have encountered the experience of these failing to achieve the form expected. The way in which something has been seen and apparently understood will change when it is expressed through a medium. This is because the medium forms an integral part of the form that response takes and will shape it significantly. For example, a print will have all the qualities of printed surfaces, shapes and colours integrated into any pictorial content and affecting its appearance. Experienced and practised artists and craftsmen will have their perceptions partly formed by the medium they use, seeing possibilities for extending their image-making both in the choice of medium as well as subject matter.[5]

Each person will perceive a given stimulus differently, some according to already existing art forms, others to predetermined expectations of how they might employ it, while others attempt to perceive the stimulus freshly. As far as children are concerned, they are so used to being told and accepting that teacher has the answers anyway, they may seldom want to question or talk about the stimulus presented to them, although talking about a stimulus is an important way of assimilating the experience. Even when they are not allowed to talk, some kind of assimilation takes place through sharing, comparing and matching. Depending on the confidence of the individual, he will start from sharing, even to the point of imitating. Later he may move away from this state into more personal work or require further stimulus.

The skill of the teacher in recognising the patterns of activity in children is paramount, for an insecure child, who may find his starting point through imitation, can be inhibited completely if attention is drawn to his copying at the wrong time.

Another way in which the initial stimulus is made personal is through direct engagement with the stimulus. This is not always easy in a classroom, but is evident when plants, animals or found objects are handled by children and they have time to 'feed' on the sensation. Direct sensory experience, involving tactile and spatial senses particularly, can be profoundly significant in strengthening, revivifying and sustaining a child's perceptions.

An extension of the notion of first-hand experience is found in the need, sometimes, for there to be an emotional impact in the stimulus offered to children. The darkening or rearrangement of part of the classroom, the combination of sounds, music, words and objects, coming together as an image, can often directly trigger a response because of the impact on the perceptions and memory of the individual.

Obviously, the stimulation of perceptions can be made more personal through direct involvement with media. The feel and response of paint can, of itself, focus an individual's perception. Yet, there comes a point when further exploratory work with a medium gradually seems to be purposeless unless it reveals new ways of giving form to one's ideas and perceptions.

Figure 6.1: Boy Painting

Placing spots of colour over a painting is an obvious way in which a child exerts maximum control over the medium. This action also happens when a child becomes dissatisfied with or frustrated by the work he/she is doing.

This condition becomes apparent when a child, for no apparent reason, dabs spots of colour or superficial decoration all over a painting which hitherto seemed to give satisfaction in the way it was developing. (See Figure 6.1, p.103.)

Another way in which perception fades is when the individual visualises just the way to do something but finds that it doesn't work out in practice. Through previous experience he has a clear idea of how to interpret the stimulus, yet the technical problems or skill with the medium forestall the looked-for result and the perception fades in frustration. The teacher can observe perception fading through careful and practised listening and watching. Therefore, at a particular moment, the teaching of a technique could not only be appropriate but act as a catalyst to the furtherance of the child's work.

(2) Knowledge or Technique May Be Lacking

This is one of the most apparent ways in which creative endeavour can be frustrated. It may not be apparent to the individual until he has struggled with an idea or attempted, and partially failed, to find a solution to the problems he encounters that his knowledge or technique may be lacking. In fact, the search for solutions can be very inventive and actually energise the creative endeavour. If the resultant forms appear messy, lacking cohesion and fail to satisfy, then for someone inexperienced the loss of confidence and interest can be devastating, but, so can the takeover of the child's own ideas by the imposition of a technique. The technique should, somehow, be insinuated into the endeavour in order to energise and release the idea. The teaching of an apparently simple technique can often result in some children being left with no hope of progress beyond the continual reference back to the teacher. A long line of children waiting to be told what to do is one effect of the dominance of technique teaching over personal endeavour and discovery. The key to achieving the looked-for progress seems to be in achieving a balance between the individual's reawakened confidence and his skill at manipulating the medium towards his idea.

Children have to be helped to see that their ideas will change as they try to develop them through a medium and that the use of specific techniques can alter considerably the development of their work.

The reason for stating the difficulty with handling technique in this way is my belief that the frustrations which exist between a child's ideas and the form they take, between what he/she wants to do and its realisation in a medium are basic and essential to creative activity. If we understand and respect this as teachers we should not circumvent the experience for children by expecting them to adopt techniques unquestioningly but help them to find relevant ways of coping with the visual and aesthetic problems that arise, whether these are technical, inventive or whatever.

(3) The Level of Skill Is Inadequate

All of us will experience inadequate levels of skill at times and this is especially so when considering young children. When a child is still in the egocentric phase of development, the skill with which he handles media will not be of such immediate concern, for the confidence, spontaneity and directness with which he expresses his responses will carry him through most of the difficulties he encounters. Even so, the care and presentation of media (clean paint and brushes, sharp pencils) and a range of appropriate tools are essential if it is believed that the aim is to raise levels of sensitivity and not just produce pieces of work.

The problem of levels of skill becomes more apparent and pressing as children leave behind their egocentricity and become capable of building concepts independently from actual experience. Thus, the ideas and images which arise in their minds may require more skill in their realisation than they have yet achieved. In this circumstance, the practising of skill can become an end in itself and a particular child can achieve some status in the group by his 'expertise' at handling a tool or medium. In every group there are some children who have developed specific skills at home or at school and, whether these are relevant or not, will want to exhibit them whenever the chance arises. Thus the intention of the teacher to obtain a piece of work from every child can be subverted by some of them finding fulfilment in manipulating media without ever visiting possible failure by attempting to finish a piece of work.

Skill can be a very ambiguous advantage in the field of creative work. Too much skill can easily lead to repetition and worthless clichés. An example might be the skill some children develop at drawing horses or cartoons. Just when the handling of a medium has been mastered the point of what is done with it seems to surface; creating a form in clay or an image in paint has to feel right and satisfy a vision or idea in the mind. Lurking beyond mere accomplishment and skilful manipulation is the personal satisfaction and pleasure in the result; the meaning of the image for the individual. The essence of the visual or visualised experience, or at least a part of it, has to be realised in the piece of art if some satisfaction is to be achieved.

This is one of the hardest experiences for children to encounter, especially during junior school age, when an understanding of the adult world can so easily become a copy or poor imitation of it. Furthermore, the approval or otherwise of other children can become a very powerful influence on what a child does and how he/she does it. 'He's good at drawing' can mean that the child receiving such approval from the group will seldom dare to risk developing his/her work differently despite the skill and potential he/she shows in a particular area.

Unlike perception and technique, which can remain in the province of those demonstrating them and outside the individual's personal accomplishment, skill must reside in the individual. Children may copy technique and go along with a teacher's perception, but they have to become involved personally if their own levels of skill are to develop. Similarly with response, it is the individual who responds, no one else can respond for him and I consider personal response next.

(4) The Response Is Lacking and 'They Have Few Ideas'

The last part of this heading has been said to me by teachers, on many occasions, sometimes rather desperately. The reasons for an apparent lack of ideas in children are complex and will arise from a matrix of influences as much as any single cause. Once again, it is not an uncommon occurence for any of us, even for practising artists, to feel bereft of ideas. It therefore seems sensible to consider some of the sources of ideas first.

The mind and the senses need to be fed and nourished as much as the physical body, except that the 'food' is all kinds of sensory — especially visual and tactile — imaginative and inventive experiences. Children can hardly avoid having such experiences, but in relation to school, the value and potential of them can be dissipated, the meaning lost and the response in the individual remain unexpressed, or only poorly so. If education is to mean anything it should be able to offer more than the random experiences picked up out of school. At least schools should offer different, perhaps more considered and thought-out, experiences to enable children to grow and progress in their development.

The expression and communication of experience is a vital part of such growth for which different opportunities are essential and among which the visual and aesthetic must rank very high. Having few ways to communicate and being able only to communicate at a certain, mundane, level of experience can lead all too easily to apathy, frustration or violence. Therefore, the first source of nourishment for ideas is their communication to others. This is especially true for children where the capacity of the listener and the appropriate and perceptive levels of question and discussion can be seen to enrich powers of expression and communication.

If a teacher seldom finds time to listen to children and share their thoughts, observations and questions, whether in their art or their speech, then the children will be ill-disposed to communicate with the teacher. They may well answer questions, talk about the things the teacher wants them to do, what the teacher suggests but seldom reveal more personal or extra-classroom experiences. It can be difficult, initially, for the teacher to get out of this impasse for he may not know what kinds of things to ask the children nor what to say about their work. It seems that such communication from children can only be discovered by listening, being quiet with and talking with (not at) them. If a teacher sees the response and ideas of children as being important (that is, more important, at a given time perhaps than many other things) then he will make opportunities for them. I have no doubt that encouraging children to communicate their interests and ideas and finding ways to discuss them, without necessarily feeling the need to act on them every time, is a significant way to stimulate ideas. Such exchanges with the teacher need not always lead to 'writing about it' or 'making a piece of art'.

We are all stimulated by, and respond to, real things, whether a shell, a plant, an environment or a person. We can take from them as many and different nuances of feeling and understanding as the memory and imagination will allow. The connections and relationships are endless and both evoke responses and are evoked by them. The means of forming responses to experience and developing ideas have to be coaxed and nurtured.

Babies and very young children need sensory stimulation and will seek it out. 'The seeking of stimulation could be seen as a basic drive', Daniel Stern suggests.[6]

It is through a rich and varied sensory experience that young children can become sensorily intelligent about the world in which they live. Such intelligence enables and directs a young child's responses so that the patterns of understanding which form in the mind are capable of more varied and adaptable behaviour. A young child who is short of such experiences is indeed deprived and the range and diversity of his development can so easily be impaired because of lack of sensory nourishment.

Older children need support and encouragement if they are to gain fully from first hand experience, for there is a focusing of attention and a heightening of awareness which, though possible without support, is more readily achieved with it. Once a state of mind is reached which can assume conceptually what something is like, the embarrassment, or lack of will actually to touch or become involved with it can get between an individual and real experience. Hence, children of junior school age may often appear diffident or insensitive when faced with real experiences and objects to touch.

In an age when so much is seen and heard at second hand and therefore 'known about', the actual contact with the familiar things of our environment can seem tame and even unrewarding. As one teacher said of her urban school in an unguarded moment: 'We haven't got any environment where we are.' Yet it is the way in which children are helped to see, and how teachers respond to that seeing which nourishes their capacity to have ideas from their environment and to respond to their experience of it.

Of course, there are many ways of recording or registering our response to the environment from the measured, diagrammatic investigation to the evocative, personal image. The further away from a mere annotation or description of something we get the more difficult it becomes to register the range of understanding and feeling inspired by the experience. It is not description which unlocks the richness of interpretation and meaning; something more is sought and needed. Children should be helped to develop a critical awareness of their own work and that of others. Such awareness arises from looking, discussing, hypothesising, speculating and questioning. Here, the work of artists and craftsmen can be of value, where children can be given the opportunity to enjoy and respond to the considered and well resolved visual statements of artists. It has already been stated that art education must be concerned particularly with the individual's growth and response to visual ideas and images. Therefore, the way in which we help children to remain visually alert and become more responsive must include looking at and talking about the work of artists. Focusing on the different aspects of a work of art and sorting out its visual elements can give children confidence and knowledge with which to develop their understanding.

The work of artists contains all the elements of ambiguity which arise between the way they portray, through their chosen medium, aspects of their reality and what may be considered objective reality as such. There exists a resonance between the constantly changing visual experiences of the world of objects, people, places, events and phenomena on the one hand and the inner world of awarenesses, sensitivities, recognitions, memories and associations on the other. We usually deal with the evocation of one experience in another through association, simile, metaphor and image. I believe that children can learn the language of such experiences and enjoy using it, given the right support by the teacher.

Of course, young children (below the age of seven) will make all kinds of associations using their language of marks and schemes to describe and symbolise their responses to the world around them. After the age of seven, the distinction between real things and made up things becomes more evident and the resonance between personal and factual reality begins.

In all these suggestions, children's responses becomes evident and the richness or poverty of their experience will be seen to determine the ideas they have and the range and diversity of response they make.

Art or Objectivity — the Dawn of Creative Awareness

Underlying all that has been introduced in this chapter is a further and central idea about art education and the experience of making art. This central idea stems from the way we see the significance of the separation between two lots of reality which begins around the age of seven.

Observation of children playing will reveal many examples of the separation which takes place after age seven between a purely egocentric view of the world and one based on conceptual understanding. After the seventh year children will discuss games and make up rules for their conduct; they will conceptualise events and possibilities in such a way that they will see how something works or fits together. Yet they will also fantasise all kinds of possibilities for the same objects to be used in their games. In other words the reality of things as such impresses itself on their awareness but they also have to make statements about such experience in their own terms.

The experience that appearance of reality cannot do more than approximate to real things is the beginning of an understanding of the ambiguity which exists between the way one sees things for oneself and how they actually are. Gradually (or sometimes over the holiday breaks) children adopt various strategies to cope with this situation. For example, they will adopt and defend a limited response in the art they produce, such as always using pencil; they will find and adapt stereotypes through copying or being led by others; they will profess an interest in a limited number of 'subjects' or, of course, they will just give up, saying 'I'm no good at art'.

Teachers will also adopt strategies for managing the difficulties which this situation presents for them. As the lack of confidence surfaces in junior school age children, teachers will cope with it by demonstrating finite, easily managed tasks; these can be simple techniques, craft-type experiences, result-directed activities, such as can be seen being demonstrated on television, copies from books as illustrations to or arising from other work, and so on.[7]

These activities, often labelled 'ideas' for things to do, can enable teachers, inexperienced in art and crafts, to cope with the problem of getting children to produce some 'art work' even though the children express a lack of confidence to do so. However, resorting to what are, in the end, gimmicks and novelty, can have an unpleasant way of being self-perpetuating; that is, the more the teacher leads from the front, telling and showing children what has to be done, the more the children expect and wait to be shown what to do. Furthermore, the scope for children to attempt some personal interpretation, different from that suggested by the teacher, is diminished. If too many children deviate from the teacher's suggestions or expectations, the very problems, which made the teacher feel uncertain and which he wished to avoid, will again surface. How do you assess and 'guide' a child's art if it deviates from the teacher's view? The children can feel inadequate to the task if this happens and there is no background of shared looking and discussion which is essential if individual ideas are to be attempted.

My observation of teachers, and discussions with them, indicate that this is an unsatisfactory state of affairs which most teachers would wish to avoid if they could. However, as soon as they present children with an opportunity to do 'their own work' the results seem so banal or obscure that the attempt seems worthless. Nevertheless, finding ways to encourage and support children to work from their own observations and ideas is of paramount importance and quite definitely the way forward if children are to grow in confidence and understanding.

Discussing art or objectivity is the way forward precisely because children meet the problem of seeing that reality is different from their conception of it. The way that real things appear in their art and the feeling that appearances of reality cannot do more than approximate to real things, is, surely, when creative awareness dawns.

It is because children move from the egocentric phase of development to one of self-awareness that they begin to experience doubts about their art. At seven and eight they still have a great curiosity about the world and their art is an important means whereby they observe and investigate the world around them. However they invent their own worlds through their play and in their art, the awareness that real things are different cannot be avoided.

Thus, the simple discovery that materials do not behave as they imagine they should or want them to behave is the beginning of a long and important series of experiences which can be called making art. For making art is one way in which we can give personal order and meaning to our complex experiences of reality. It starts with the notions that materials create their own peculiar shapes, appearances and form and that we are not and perhaps never can copy what we see but have to find our own ways of interpreting it.

It is for this reason, above all others, that teachers have to find ways to discuss the forms of art and visual expression. Between our ideas and their expression, between the imaginative vision and the form it takes in some material, there exists a tension which has to be resolved. The resolution is not in terms of copy or description but image, metaphor and interpretation. Every time a teacher finds a way to discuss the visual and aesthetic qualities of a child's work rather than its descriptive content, he is developing the child's power to find his own expressive forms and understand those of others. It is this idea which underlies the task of teaching art and the next chapter will look at this task in more detail.

To summarise, this chapter considered the changes which come about in teaching as the basis for learning moves from one that is knowledge-based to an experiential one. The effects of this shift require new ways of looking at the role of the teacher in relation to children's learning and the chapter suggests a basis for doing this in regard to art education. Certain key relationships between perception and response, technique and skill are discussed. Underlying these observations is the central concern of art education, that of understanding the difference between description and interpretation. It is proposed that the dawn of creative awareness arises from this distinction and that the central task of the teacher lies in helping children to grow in confidence and understanding to meet this challenge.

Notes

1. Robin Tanner, a practising etcher; formerly Art Adviser for Oxfordshire.
2. Marion Richardson, *Art and the Child* (University of London Press, 1948).
3. Viktor Lowenfeld, *The Lowenfeld Lectures*, edited by John Michael (Pennsylvania State University Press, 1982), pp.33-4.
4. Elliott Eisner, *Educating Artistic Vision* (Collier, Macmillan, 1972), p. 9.
5. Ibid., p. 96.
6. See Seonaid Robertson, *Rosegarden and Labyrinth* (Routledge and Kegan Paul, 1963), p. 21.
7. Daniel Stern, *The First Relationship: Infant and Mother* (Fontana, Opea Books, 1977), pp. 61-2.
8. See Victor D'Amico, *Creative Teaching in Art* (International Textbook Co. 1953), p. 4.

7 A POSSIBLE APPROACH TO TEACHING ART

Heightened sensitivity and creative awareness, as central issues in the teaching of art, may appear difficult to specify and even more tricky to recognise and describe. Nevertheless, it must be possible to create conditions which engender an atmosphere which make it more, rather than less, possible for those things to exist. It is obvious that our understanding and perception of sensitivity and creative awareness depend rather largely on what we as teachers bring to each situation. Our values, the perspective from which we view children's learning and the importance we place on an individual's way of seeing and understanding all matter.

Teachers have to work hard to maintain their integrity and their quality of observation of how children learn. Both of these things, in my view, are important in the work of a teacher whatever the subject, but are essential in teaching art.

In attempting to describe alternative classroom practices, an approach is suggested here which aims to bring into practical focus the issues raised in the previous chapter.

At the risk of putting my head on the block, I will attempt to set out a possible approach to the teaching of art. This approach, based on the ideas in the previous chapter, will be aimed at the five to thirteen age group but may also have implications for the way art education is conceived with older pupils.

The underlying assumption is that the central aim of teaching art is to raise children's levels of sensitivity to visual and aesthetic qualities and heighten their creative and critical awareness of art forms. In terms of art teaching these are understood as sensitivity to media, to appearances, arrangements and relationships occurring naturally, and man-made, and a creative and critical awareness of the visual ideas and meanings they promote. These developments would extend from the images and forms in their own work to those of others and could include the work of artists and craftsman in their own and other cultures.

In practice, this central aim would have to be realised through a number of objectives which are essential to the making and appreciation of art. These objectives can be grouped in four broad, related and interdependent areas, each one providing a vital aspect of art experience. The four areas of objectives I suggest are:

(1) Stimulating and heightening perception, including critical awareness and its associated vocabulary.

(2) Developing the capacity to respond to and communicate ideas visually and spatially.

(3) Developing and practising appropriate skills, both practical and critical.

(4) Learning, devising, inventing and applying techniques and acquiring knowledge.

In considering the following examples we should be aware of these objectives being evident in the work of the teachers. In one case they are not specified, and an imbalance exists between the teacher's aims and the children's responses. In the second, the continual interaction between teacher and taught comes about because the teacher is mindful that he is responsible for much more than getting children to produce pieces of art; he is aware of the broader objectives that are necessary to fulfil his aim.

Thus the raising of levels of visual and aesthetic sensitivity is seen as a central, underpinning aim of art teaching from which other aims might arise and within which the objectives for particular pieces of work will be formulated. In order to understand how this aim might affect teaching art in practice, I will endeavour to formulate two examples of the different directions in which two approaches to teaching might go. Although, inevitably, these examples will be full of assumptions, they are used to contextualise specific points about teaching from an aim rather than assuming that aims are self-evident in practice.

Example A. In the first instance the teacher does not specify any real objectives for the work he wishes the children to do and there is only the vague aim, perhaps just a hope, that some nice pictures will result. For this particular session powder paint is the chosen medium and it is to be related to the stimulus of some flowers which he has brought into the classroom.

The teacher talks to the children as a group about the flowers, pointing out certain of their features and particularly the quality of their colour. He asks questions about mixing certain hues and supplies answers where none is forthcoming from the children. He shows satisfaction when he receives anticipated answers. However, some answers and observations by the children are difficult to deal with as they are unexpected or appear inappropriate. These he ignores, parries with another question or shows some irritation as the child does not appear to be listening nor following the trend of his argument. Come what may, he does not allow himself to be deflected from the purpose he has in mind, namely the production of acceptable flower paintings.

Immediately the children start work some of them begin to find difficulty with the paint, both in mixing it with water and mixing colours together. Then there are others who have started making elaborate and, in a few cases, skilful drawings in pencil. The teacher knows from past encounters that there will be problems when these children come to paint, and these are problems he finds difficult to solve. Yet other children seem to be really enjoying the powder paint, mixing quantities of colour and covering the paper with a zest that, for a while, shows obvious pleasure. Unfortunately for the teacher, some of these children seem to have forgotten the topic, as the colours they are mixing bear no relation to the flowers they are supposed to be painting. Other children don't appear to know how to start at all.

The teacher senses the situation and moves amongst the class encouraging them in their work, cajoling some, restraining others, attempting to get the children to look at the flowers and produce at least some approximation to them. In doing this he is clearly responding to the dynamic development of learning rather than accepting a linear one, even though he is still attempting to maintain the direction of their work towards the production of flower paintings. He begins to feel that whatever direction individual pieces of work go in, if a child is purposefully engaged and obviously trying, it is better for as many as possible to produce something than criticise them for not doing what he intended.

As the session progresses, the chances of more than, say, a third of the children producing an acceptable flower painting recede, and the hope or vague aim of the teacher has to be modified. It seems once again that those who can draw or those who have a natural facility with paint are the successful ones; the others will have had varying degrees of satisfaction but realise, one way or another, that their work is not acceptable. To conclude the session the teacher extracts the most acceptable flower paintings and talks about these and feels that at least some of the children have understood what he wanted them to do.

The relaxation, the lack of pressure and, for some, the creative satisfaction make the art time a period to be looked forward to and enjoyed. It is as much this attitude and the response of the children, as any objective criteria, that make the teacher feel it is worthwhile; in any case he asserts that they are all individuals and their work, to a more or less degree, is an expression of that individuality. It is difficult to conceive any objective way of assessing the worth of what is done and progress seems difficult to judge except as far as the worth of individual pieces of work goes.

There are a number of difficulties inherent in this approach to teaching art which I will try to bring out. Subsequently I will attempt to suggest possible answers to the problems raised here in my second example.

The first difficulty is that the interaction between teacher, children and the work does not enable an intelligent awareness to develop about using media and making visual statements. The act of making art, like that of teaching, remains a hit and miss, rather subjective business. As such this leaves the teacher, the children and their work prey to any opinion, any criteria and any assumptions that may be made for them. Although it could be said that he engaged the children in some of the objectives, this was in a random and rather subjective way. For example, he stimulated their perceptions (of flowers in this instance) but, because he found it difficult to manage the range of their responses, did little to heighten these perceptions further or introduce a critical vocabulary.

Similarly, some skills will have developed but not had the space to become individual or inventive in terms of the techniques children were able to devise for themselves.

Secondly, the teacher has not taught by relating to and extending the children's experience; he has brought into focus, drawn attention to and made significant only those aspects of the experience he sees and knows and found no way in which to enlist the experiences and observations of the children. He has not injected into the experience of paint and flowers anything that is likely to give the children a different basis for creating and looking other than that to which he directs them or, by chance, they may already have acquired.

Thirdly, he has not encouraged language, nor shared or explored ways of talking about painting, thus providing no opportunity for critical awareness to develop. He has provided no clues for assessing the merits of the work done. Therefore, the sensitivity and intelligence of the children concerning painting remains ambivalent and leaves no basis on which to build further experience.

The irony is that the teacher, in this case, may never be wrong in his assessment of worth because he has specified no aims against which to appraise it and every judgement is subjective. However, this also means that he can never be right, if that is the best way of putting it. If it is the understanding, awareness and range of sensitivity of the children which the teacher is attempting to change, then he must find ways to build up a vocabulary about these matters and wherever possible enable children to share any evidence of this happening in their work. To have no aims other than those which might subjectively emerge from the work is clearly no way to educate, nor to build up experience for possible future development.

Example B. Perhaps we should now consider the second instance of teaching and the alternatives it suggests. In this case, the teacher wishes the children to paint but makes the professional judgement that many of them may find difficulty in handling the powder paint. Therefore his immediate objective towards the central aim of raising levels of sensitivity to visual and aesthetic experiences is to help the children understand the nature of the medium of paint. They are first encouraged to handle it as a substance rather than a colouring agent, exploring its characteristics and ways of behaving.

The teacher shows and/or talks sufficiently to initiate some exploratory activity by the children, recognising that many of them will not see the point of the activity beyond enjoying it and others will not understand what they are supposed to do.

However, the teacher has thought it essential to provide really clean paint, clean water, at least one pot between two children, and clean brushes of different sizes together with small pieces of paper. The latter ensures that explorations are of a short duration and not laboured.

As the children begin to handle the medium, the teacher watches and listens carefully, intervening only when asked to or if excessive or silly behaviour threatens to interfere with someone else. He feels no need to direct or justify the exploration which is going on. Some children will explore the paint a little, others, not knowing what is expected of them, will copy each other, others will do what they have always done and yet others will try to draw with the brush or make patterns.

The teacher watches all this happening and when the activity and noise level indicates that attention is waning generally, even if this is after a very short while, he stops the class in order to look at and share with the group the results of this first exploration.

Through a series of observations, questions and discussion about the appearance and behaviour of paint, the teacher will endeavour to increase the children's understanding and vocabulary to do with paint. Many, of course, may not as yet have found out very much, but this ploy is used to share round the experience and enlarge each child's view of what is expected through shared example. Intelligence about paint must arise through handling it, through trying to find words to talk about it and through looking at and sharing the experience of others.

The teacher will now talk with the children about what has emerged from the experience of 'exploring the paint'. He will realise that different starting points and areas of difficulty have become apparent as the work has progressed. Some children found it difficult to understand the teacher's perception of the task and needed further explanation which, when it was not forthcoming, led them to copy other children. Some children responded immediately and wanted to handle the paint straight away. Others wondered how to mix the colour, how much water to use, which brush and how many colours. Yet other children seemed to revel in the substance of the paint and enjoy mixing it and playing with it, hardly seeming to be interested in the marks they made beyond the skill of handling it. Each of these groups would be experiencing something rather different and require more or less intervention by the teacher.

However, the immediate objective was to establish some common experiences collectively, which would enable the children to understand more what was wanted of them. The teacher will now impress on the children what has emerged as 'exploring the paint' — perhaps to the point of showing how to mix the colour if this appears necessary — and exhort them to continue with the work. It will be assumed that before long, many children will try to control the paint in various ways and not just through the way paint is mixed with water and applied to the paper. These ways of control could include the following: drawing a picture, object or pattern, making patterns and symmetries from the brush strokes, applying the paint methodically to the paper and tilting the paper to control wet paint.

When the teacher observes this beginning to happen, other tools for controlling paint can be given to some children — pieces of card, sticks, sponges, palette knives and so on. As the children's explorations and ways of control proceed, the task of the teacher is to keep the level of awareness of what is happening as high as possible. Once again, as the concentration changes and the noise level with it, it will be time to look at the range of discoveries that have been made. This time there will be much more to talk about as the children have made their own discoveries.

Now, the discussion and observation will be that much more informed. The experience will have been satisfactory for most children because the emphasis has been centred on the actual experience of paint and not on how clever some children are at drawing or pattern making, nor on the opinion and intervention of the teacher. The more this engagement with children's actual experience and response continues, the more confidence they will feel in the way they handle the medium and talk about it.

What happens next depends on the way a particular group of children and a particular teacher interact. Arising from their looking and discussion, ideas and suggestions will develop which could be followed up in various ways. The characteristic of ideas at this age (post seven to junior school) is that they may lead in different directions, but will also be shared, copied and promote collaboration. The teacher might interleave his ideas with the children's, perhaps showing them paintings by artists whose work has a similar exploratory approach. He may also provide appropriate stimuli which relate, in their visual possibilities, to the kinds of discoveries children are already making. In other words, he will attempt to reinforce and focus the underlying aim of art teaching, namely the sensitivity with which the medium has been handled and the awareness of the forms it provides which promote aesthetic sensitivity. He will realise that such an aim is not achieved overnight and will require the patient preparation and collaboration which have become part of his approach.

Throughout his work with the children, the interaction between the four areas of objectives is obvious. He has purposefully engaged children's ideas and observed responses; he has built on and developed language through discussion and questioning and also encouraged children to work in their own way. As we will see in Chapter 11, this teacher has the basis for a significant and useful form of assessment of what the children do in art.

There will be some children who, as in the previous example, will not have produced very much to look at. Yet it should be possible to relate whatever they may have done to the work of the group and the underpinning aim of the work. This is because results taken as an aim can be interpreted at any level and include a whole range of results. In other words, sensitivity to paint and painted images is inclusive of any experience with paint, whereas a picture of something only includes other work which approximates to the same notion of picture. Clearly, the aim of raising levels of visual and aesthetic sensitivity is achieved more readily by sensing the dynamic growth of children's actual experience in making art than by sticking to a linear development towards narrowly specified ends.

In the two examples given, the teacher in the second one had thought about what children should learn from the experiences he provided and related this learning to his observation of them at work. He wanted them to understand and was confident enough to engage them in discussion about their work. The teacher in the first example had no real aims and focused his intentions for the children's work on an end result. There was no real thought about what the children were supposed to learn and therefore little for him to share with them other than his opinion of which results were best.

Perhaps another way of looking at the difference between the approach of these two teachers and between a linear and a dynamic approach to teaching is to consider the working atmosphere and kind of environment generated in each case.

Creating the Atmosphere for Teaching Art

Of all the things which affect the way in which children learn, the most pervasive yet difficult to describe is the atmosphere which exists in a school, and especially a classroom. The atmosphere is particularly telling where children are expected to commit themselves in a personal way and where their responses and ideas can be exposed to the view of others, as in art. Although we may recognise and respond to different qualities of atmosphere in a school or classroom it is not so easy to say how they arise.

In one sense atmosphere is contributed to by the physical arrangements, environmental conditions and appearances of a particular building or classroom. If it is hemmed in, run down, badly maintained and lacking in any pleasing visual features, a school or classroom will require so much more effort to make it into a place where children want to be. Yet we will all have been to schools in very impoverished areas which somehow have become oases in the surrounding desert. Likewise, an uninspiring and lack-lustre classroom can be transformed by a change of teacher. We can all recognise the differences between the physical conditions of different places and see the different provision which is being made, yet we know in our hearts that there is more to creating the right atmosphere than improving physical things; these will contribute to the context but are not the main cause.

Perhaps more importantly, it is to do with the way people behave towards each other, the expectations they have for and of each other, the language they adopt, the gestures and expressions they unconsciously use and so on. It seems, therefore, that the notion of atmosphere, about which I wish to write, arises from a collection of attitudes, expectations, beliefs and working approaches as much as physical arrangements or material provision.

Some teachers create an atmosphere within which children seem to work with a purpose, identification and autonomy which seems almost entirely lacking and unattainable by others. It would be possible to find two teachers, working in similar conditions, achieving totally different outcomes despite the dedication and hard work they both employ. The balance between teacher and pupil initiatives, between acceptance and rejection of individual ideas, the values placed on some activities rather than others, the use made of completed work — the list could go on — are the kinds of differences which might emerge. The subtle shifts which take place in these balances both create and are sustained by the atmosphere in a classroom. For example, a teacher who wanted to improve the manner in which work was finished off might use completed work competitively or comparatively, whereas another teacher might use it for discussion and personal enquiry. Both teachers could have the same aim but their different stances would have considerably different effects on the atmosphere in which children learnt. In the first instance the different results of endeavour by the pupils would be emphasised; in the second the understanding and discoveries, of which the results were some embodiment, would be the focus.

The subtle shifts which take place in these various balances both create and are sustained by the atmosphere in the classroom. I want to examine the way in which this happens and attempt to bring into focus aspects of practice which help rather than hinder the creating of a positive, working atmosphere in a classroom.

In order to do this I will describe the approach and work of two teachers, in the hope that the underlying issues will be manifest and the differences between a dynamic and a linear approach become manifest. Thus, the matrix which individuals create is rather like a net which allows certain things to be caught while others fall through.

For example, the confidence of children to formulate and ask their own questions, to seek answers from sources other than the teacher and to try out different solutions to problems they encounter may be one aspect of learning which slips through the matrix created by one teacher but is caught by another. My supposition is that this is because one teacher has a more linear, result-orientated view of teaching than another who is prepared to accept a more dynamic and experiential view. Their different aims, if formulated, are likely to suggest this difference.

If we pursue this particular example it may be possible to deduce some of the things which inhibit or enable confidence to grow in children to ask questions and try out their own solutions.

Example C. In the first example the teacher provides interest displays of objects, to be looked at rather than handled, some of which are to be the stimulus for children's art work. Work, which is already mounted on the wall, is not there for discussion or comment but as a final, selected repository of the best work done and to make the room look finished. Displayed work is always mounted in an average but similar way, whether this is appropriate or not. Sometimes the shapes of children's drawings and paintings are cut round and remounted; the teacher makes use of assorted, brightly coloured paper and often sets work at different angles to give variety to the displays. Unfortunately all this effort on his part serves only to emphasise the teacher's work on display rather than the subtlety of the children's pieces.

Books and equipment tend to have their place in boxes on shelves or in cupboards and are accessible more to the teacher than to the children. This creates circumstances requiring him to spend time giving out and taking in the things children need. Corners around which children cannot be seen, even if they could be trusted, are avoided. There is a feeling, often transmitted through comments and asides, that children who are not producing or constantly working at something are, in fact, not working at all. One consequence of this underlying attitude is that leaving things out, whether in displays, materials from which to work, or pieces that are still in the process of completion, is not tolerated easily. Furthermore, children are not given the responsibility to tidy away and keep in order the materials and media they use, so that clearing up is either done by favourites or under some duress, rather than from their own volition. Busy activity is promoted as work; and such things as questions, discussion and reflection are not.

Most of the art work is generated from the front of the class by the teacher giving hints, methods, directions and demonstrations with the implication that every child should attempt to follow them. Rhetorical questions steer the more wayward children towards the common task and any observations, remarks or questions raised by children which fall outside the teacher's limited purpose are either ignored or turned aside in favour of his theme.

There is an air of evasion or vague encouragement from the teacher in response to the work children do which does not fit his expectations. He is uncomfortable when faced with unusual or unpredictable responses which he tends to discourage and discount. In fact, the teacher already knows which children will not make much of a job of the work he has initiated and those who will produce 'good' or passable results. Some children feel secure in activity sessions because they know what is expected of them as possible work — good, bad or indifferent though this may be. Others feel that they are no good at art and doubt whether they ever will be.

The time allocated for art is not just something which he is expected to provide, for he feels that most of the children like the art time and there is a pleasant and often relaxed feeling about it and, further, it is a good way to spend an afternoon when the more basic work is completed. Very occasionally he has used the anticipation of the art session as a means of coercion to get other work done. Basically, though, he feels that this is not quite fair as some of the 'good' artists are children who do not shine at anything else. He justifies the time spent on art activity to himself and, if pressed, to others who may visit his room, by the quality of work arising from the few who do well at the task in his terms and the general feeling of relaxed good will.

This teacher's aims tend to be couched in terms of things to do which seldom have any connection between them even when they purport to follow a common theme and his approach, although friendly and encouraging, is still linear and result-orientated. For example, themes and ideas for art may come from history, with drawings arising from the text, or from nature study, with paintings of plants which illustrate the subject; but such work never illuminates the children's understanding and seldom raises their visual and aesthetic sensitivity in any conscious way. There is no sense of a child's discoveries with colour being used in a relevant way to extend their awareness of historical costume or plant growth. There is no thought of enlarging the children's visual vocabulary but a bland acceptance of book illustration stereotypes or the direct description of presented objects.

This approach has the dual effect of promoting a demand from the children for new or novel things to do — with the comment 'We've done that already sir' being the most unnerving — and an increasingly desperate search for things to do on the part of the teacher. This search can occupy time and energy that is more appropriately required in other ways such as keeping materials and media in good order, finding interesting stimuli or relating positively to the things children are creating.

This teacher works hard at the demands generated by the children and by his own approach. He is delighted and satisfied when the children produce work he likes, yet underneath all this effort there is an undoubted impression that the art the children produce is bitty, disconnected and rather lacking in direction.

The positive, often dogmatic approach of the teacher masks an insecurity about the real point of doing art and an uncertainty about what the children ought to be doing. Victor D'Amico describes this state of teaching.[1]

The matrix of approaches, expectations and beliefs of this teacher, which create the atmosphere within which children learn, will obviously allow certain things to flourish while others are inhibited. For example, it is unlikely that children will feel confident to work in ways different from those suggested by the teacher. They will be more inclined to wait to be told than work from their own volition. Art activities will seem less important, although enjoyable and relaxing, when compared to other school work. Their view of what art is about would be as narrow as the teacher's, and possibly as shallow in experience, were it not for some children who learned other things through copying, tracing and practising outside the classroom and at home. That art is a matter of opinion, taste and even whim, will be self-evident from the way it is actually treated by the teacher, despite his wish to do otherwise.

Somehow, the children are given no firm ground from which to view art experience because there are only the vague uncertainties of the teacher and the continual round of new things they are told to do. Perhaps there are just those who are good at art and those who never will be.

Such an atmosphere is unstable, lacking in positive educational support, mistrusting of what children can do and want to do, and often reduces art to an illustrative, gimmicky and pastime activity. I believe that underlying all these effects is the basic difficulty of finding a structure of ideas that enable the children's responses, ideas, observations and so on, to be related to the teacher's purposes. This is why it is important to understand the dynamic approach, not as a model, but as a way of describing what happens in practice. In this light, children's questions, observations and ways of doing things, will be seen to have a direct relationship to the work they produce and be a strong argument for it.

Example D. If we now take a further example, it will be possible to see that the atmosphere created will allow art activity to develop in a different way and that the approach to teaching children is one of working in a dynamic and not linear way.

The teacher in this example also provides interest displays which are changed from time to time during each term. Changes are brought about by his observation of the way children respond to them, by children adding their own contributions or by the value of the display having been exhausted in some way. The work mounted on the wall shows a variety of approaches with some pieces being carefully double-mounted to isolate them from surrounding work, while other work is grouped on large sheets and carefully titled. A teaching point is made with some pieces which the teacher discusses with the children. One set of prints shows clearly a concern with texture and surfaces and these are adjacent to some wax rubbings which exemplify the same area of experience. The teacher refers to these in response to an observation from a child. All the work, however mounted, is carefully aligned by horizontal and vertical axes, and the edges of the board are aligned to the overall pattern which all the pieces make. Colours of mounts are generally subdued and even grey on white mounts are used to show up, but not dominate, some delicate pencil drawings (see Chapter 10).

Books and materials are easily accessible to children and they are expected to put them away and keep them tidy. This is important because the children are expected to settle down to some kind of drawing or writing and occasionally painting and clay modelling first thing in the morning and this has to be tidied away in preparation for other work. Generally, every child knows where to find the basic materials so that he/she can work at some kind of visual or written piece. The routine is such that the children know they will be expected to work in groups or with the teacher after mid-morning, but the first part of the day is for them. The teacher is active with individuals or groups that may develop if there is an interest centre. Comments and discussions on the art work being done develop during the course of the morning. Sometimes the teacher will call everyone to share in some discovery or observation. There is a feeling of tolerance and trust in the capacity of children to accept responsibility and although this does not always work in the way children behave, the teacher feels that the underlying attitude is worth the misdemeanours which sometimes occur. The room is arranged so that for some of the time it is possible for a few children to be apart from others, so that pieces of art work, which require more time to be completed, can be continued without interfering with the main group.

Although there are occasions when the teacher works from the front of the class, these are used to share ideas and exchange views on specific topics. Often small groups will spend time with the teacher while others get on with the work in hand. Always the teacher attempts to draw together the work of the day before children depart. This time is considered a special pleasure when each other's work can be looked at and talked about; when comparisons and similarities are discovered and new things discussed, often fresh directions emerge, or things to be attempted the following day. There is a general exchange which the teacher feels benefits everyone because the level at which they all work and talk can be extended. Suggestions for completing work arise and ideas about how it could be displayed.

Before this teacher started these group sessions at the end of the day he had doubts as to whether he would know what to say and about his ability to sustain them. Yet, he believed that the way ideas, observations and discoveries, are shared is essential if the work is to progress. However, discussions proved to be self-perpetuating and generate all kinds of ways to look at and understand children's art which had not occurred to him. His capacity to help children and to develop their understanding of their work seemed to grow because of these sessions.

Because so many of the children seemed able to work on their own with increasing confidence, the teacher was, to some extent, released from the continual demands made on him by them. This enabled him to spend time listening to and observing the way children worked: how they were frustrated by a lack of skill or know-how, or needed to talk about their ideas before committing them to paper. He could see, sometimes vividly, where he was needed and at other times where his intervention was really an intrusion. In fact, he began to realise that it was his knowledge of how children actually work which was vital and not his repertoire of things to give them to do. He was surprised by the innovations and discoveries some children made, by the way they sustained their work and particularly by the depth to which they went through the continual handling of a few materials. In fact, the teacher's own knowledge and confidence grew because of the discoveries of the children and his openness to their way of working. He had begun to teach through the dynamic interaction of the group and realise something of the processes involved in making art.

Yet it was not easy, as he felt the need to acquire more experience in depth of the media the children were using and he felt that his skill and knowledge were inadequate to meet their continually developing needs. Nevertheless, he felt that the purposes of children making art were becoming clearer in what he observed them doing.

The children as a group were becoming more observant and developing the visual and verbal language to communicate what they saw. The teacher had begun to keep, or to record, much of the work the children produced and become aware of certain strengths, inclinations and aptitudes which were only evident when work was seen or discussed with the child over a period of time.

He started to get the children familiar with using drawing books at odd times during the day and also used these collections of drawings as part of his record of their art work. He had become aware of the children who never produced any art work of a really personal kind and also those whose ideas and interests never seem to command attention. More children than he imagined needed support to gain the confidence to communicate, both in words, and through their art. His collections of children's work and notes began to reveal different ways of looking at progress and assessing development, from the quality and kind of observation children made to the skills they acquired in handling media.

The teacher now began to reconsider the aims of what he was doing in art. His observations of children working and his reflections on what was produced led him to formulate aims that seem more compatible with his observations and less general and vague than those he had previously held. In fact, the aims, now that they were becoming more precise, helped him to give direction and even a feeling of continuity to what the children did. For example, there was the notion of children communicating. He knew that some found it difficult with words yet had begun to convey a great deal through their drawing. Even these children talked more than before once their drawing work was being discussed and shared with others. Therefore it seemed that one of the aims must be to do with communication and with this idea in mind, a chain of thought, action and reflection was initiated. This process of observing and thinking through ideas and aims never seemed to dry up and became very productive as a way of conceiving possible new developments in the art his group of children did.

The matrix of approaches, expectations and beliefs, of this teacher, which create the atmosphere within which the children learn about art, will 'catch' quite different things from the previous example. It is likely that children will not feel threatened when their work is shared and discussed. They are likely to feel a sense of responsibility for their own and others' work and develop the capacity to talk about and plan what they do. There will be moments when they lack ideas and direction but these can be discussed because they are the kind of issues which are shared. Gradually the understanding which they acquire of a particular medium will grow in depth and affect the range and quality of work they undertake. In fact, the teacher and children between them build up a power to manipulate various media; to invent, construct, organise and express all kinds of ideas, observations and experiences.

Such an atmosphere is accepting and supportive of personal ideas and idiosyncrasies yet rigorous in the way it is organised and what is expected of each one to keep it so. There is a feeling of purpose because of the amount of sharing and discussion. Every child's work has the chance of being taken seriously, seldom is any dismissed. The children's natural inclination to talk about their work while they are doing it is linked to providing a vocabulary in group and class sessions, when their work is looked at, together with that of artists and craftsmen. There is a general and pervasive raising of intelligence about visual matters and a willingness to share views and ideas which arise from each other's knowledge and discoveries. Everyone can feel involved even if he is not always successful.

The children in Example D will have a much better basis from which to develop confidence and understanding of the form/content tension. Through the discussions and the trust they have been shown in making their own judgements, these children will begin to realise that art is not just about making representational copies and that there are many different qualities which go into a piece of art. Colour, shape, arrangement, pattern or texture are qualities for which some individuals have a natural feeling; others will respond in the way they see things, distort or exaggerate them, choose particular viewpoints and so on. Some children will find a greater affinity with one material rather than another. Underlying all these discoveries will be a growing awareness that art is to do with how individuals begin to see and interpret reality, not copy it.

Through these two examples I have tried to bring into focus the way in which the classroom atmosphere depends on so many inter-related factors in the teaching situation. Furthermore, that it is this inter-relationship, as much as any single aspect, that creates the atmosphere conducive to children producing their own art, and the teacher's ability to trust them to do so. It may be helpful if I now set down some practical aspects of these relationships and reconsider the ideas and attitudes which are helpful in building a good working atmosphere.

Practical Matters

Every teaching situation imposes its limitations and has its difficulties: we have to recognise those that we can change, adapt or modify, and those which are beyond our influence or power to alter. For example, we cannot easily change a headteacher or rebuild the school but we can find ways of talking about and showing what children can do and ways of improving the arrangement and appearance of the classroom.

The arrangement of a given room-space can be considered in

relation to sources of light, available storage and facilities like a sink and power points. The first appearance matters as this is what greets each one who enters. Tops of cupboards, window-sills and ledges should be kept clear of unsightly accumulations. Displays can be just as effective if arranged simply, and horizontals and verticals maintained in wall displays. Colour is important and should be used simply as a means for enriching and heightening appearances rather than dominating them or distracting from them. The materials and objects used in display can bring out many visual and imaginative qualities such as shape, light, texture, form, silhouette and relationship. They can also inform or evoke cultural or historical associations. The range and variety of displays will grow as the collections and sources of things to display increase and the children add to and use them.

When arranging a classroom ease of movement for teacher and pupils should be considered, in relation to storage, accessibility of materials and resources, and natural focal points such as doors, sinks, blackboards and windows. Such different activities as looking at and sharing, handling materials of different kinds, working in groups, or using books, will determine different arrangements of space and movement. Materials can be selected and stored in such a way that those for everyday use have a clearly marked, accessible place separate from stock and specialised items.

The more restricted the space and tighter the budget, the more care and selection is needed in these matters. It is better to have quality materials and tools for a restricted range of activities than poor ones for lots. The inventiveness and variety that grows from working with a few carefully chosen materials is easier to manage and educationally more effective than attempting to work with a large variety of materials.

The routines which the teacher establishes with children for collecting, cleaning and clearing away materials and media need to be established and adhered to as part of the expected way of working. Care of work produced and of work in progress is one of the bonuses of effective routines. Good working habits are most important and pervade everything that is achieved.

Underlying all these suggestions there are certain principles which it seems worth noting.

(1) The children should be helped towards personal and group responsibility for the way in which they use the room and its

resources. The trust of the teacher in the capacity of the children to work at their own ideas and thus to achieve some autonomy over what they do will grow as readily from the way children show responsibility in practical matters as from some romanticised ideal about their need for expressive freedom.

(2) The teacher should find time to observe children working and to listen to them and not have all his energy absorbed by organisational and disciplinary matters. Even a small proportion of his time spent in this way, as well as the more normal interaction with groups and individuals, will show enormous dividends.

(3) Careful organisation and planning in the work to be done and the likely materials to be used generates a feeling of purpose and makes it easier to deal with problems of disinterest and lack of confidence whch can so easily disrupt the ordered atmosphere of the class. Planning should make flexibility more possible.

(4) Careful selection and good maintenance of materials goes a long way toward helping children develop sensitivity in the work they do with art materials and media.

(5) Finding ways for children to share their work with the teacher and each other enables the teacher to focus attention on the qualities and understandings which arise from his aims. It can also create the circumstances to include work from many children, thus extending their understanding of art and increasing their confidence. Such sessions can also promote further ideas to be pursued.

(6) Some time set aside, however minimal, to observe how children work, the time and space they need, and the different aspects of their experience, is most valuable. Some analysis of the areas into which children's activity falls may be worth attempting, as has been suggested in this and the last chapter, i.e. perceptual and critical awareness, knowledge and technical understanding, response and ideas and, lastly, skills.

Working Strategies

Every time a teacher tells a child what to do and how to do it and expects the child to follow his instructions, he makes it less easy for a child to have confidence to work in his own way. Furthermore, it is likely to confirm the pattern of work in which the teacher is expected to provide the instructions and ideas for what to do. Yet this cannot be satisfactory if we believe that the child needs to explore the medium in his own way in order to discover appropriate ways of controlling it.

It is my contention that the point of children making art is that it is a means for them to communicate their ideas and understandings and to express their responses and visions. If we wish this to happen then we have to evolve strategies and ways of working that make it more and not less likely. What could some of these be?

First, we have to find ways that make looking and touching an enjoyable and purposeful activity and one that can be shared and talked about. The way in which we think through what we are going to do, and prepare the materials required to do it, is an integral part of the way in which we prepare ourselves to help children learn. Ideas arise about how to approach teaching when we ourselves handle objects and materials and imagine how children might learn from them. This helps us to be more explicit about our intentions and language concerning, for example, the visual qualities and appearances of objects.

For example, supposing we find a piece of drift-wood which attracts us, we should be able to share it with the children in such a way that attention is focused on its visual and spatial qualities as much as its description as a piece of old wood. Shape, colour, texture, pattern, or whatever else may have been the point of visual or tactile interest for us, can be shared with children and elicit their own response in kind. It is especially important for the teacher to attempt to do this if he expects the children to make some kind of visual response themselves to the object. Whatever the outcome, the teacher can use the same vocabulary when looking at and talking about children's art work as he did to talk about the piece of drift-wood.

Secondly, therefore, we have to show respect for the ideas, information and understandings of children in the way we listen to them, observe their actions, and respond to their observations. We have to attempt to do this in such a way that we do not foreclose on things that interest them or commit ourselves too much to the kind of results we expect before there has been some open and full exchange which encourages everyone to participate. It is part of the skill of the teacher to sense where and how the observations and understanding of children can relate to the educational purposes he has in mind. It must be remembered that an aim can be interpreted in many ways but a method or looked-for result invariably inhibits and excludes those whose work does not conform to it in some respect.

Thirdly, we have to leave ourselves room to make mistakes, to ask our own questions, to learn from the children and see things in different ways. In one sense this happens when we get to know children. Our knowledge of them leads us in the direction of tolerance and helps us to cope with diversity. For example, we may want certain things from a group of children which, by development, experience, background or ability, they cannot give us. This does not mean that these children fail or can make no personal contribution to the work we want them to follow. It is by searching out each one's worth and finding out what he can best contribute, at whatever level, that their confidence can be increased. The mixing of colour, the handling of pattern, an eye for detail, a developed perception of space, are examples of the kinds of things we can notice when we cease to be bemused by representation and really look at what children can do. This approach does not mean that the teacher abandons the general purpose of the work but, with the children, explores different ways of achieving it.

Fourthly, it is important to observe children while they are working, as well as moving about and helping them in groups or individually. The approach to and rhythm of work can be very different for different individuals. During the course of our observations we should note happenings, incidents, ways of working and the way work changes and develops so that we can use these findings to help children develop an intelligent and understanding attitude towards making art. I remember three eleven-year-old boys in a secondary school working at a colour mixing task set by the teacher. They were not sure of the value of it but worked with great vigour and enjoyment. Having arrived quickly at some interesting colours they didn't know what to do next. The teacher was unaware of the stage they had reached. They then worked on over and over the paper until the whole experience became tiresome and developed into a game. It was only when water was spilt that the teacher paid real attention to them. If the teacher could have been there to see and share their original revelations of colour, much could have been done to make the point of his teaching. Had he been there too soon he could have stifled it. We have to judge the response, involvement, uncertainty, confidence and so on, as children work. Sometimes it is valuable to share something with the whole group as it arises and to enable us to do this we should attempt to be aware of the quality of energy that is going into the work in hand.

Lastly, ways in which to share what children have done will be evolved by each teacher according to his/her approach and personality. What is certain is that learning about sharing work with children comes about through doing it and not thinking about it.

There is much that can be shared in children's art work without asking for direct explanations or using rhetorical questions. Perceptions about the child's point of view, difficulties he may have encountered, details he may have noticed or satisfaction in using the medium, come about because the teacher is prepared to tune into and listen to the child.

Careful observation of children working, or, if this activity is not possible, a close look at any work produced, reveals unexpected possibilities for discussion and exchange. For example, the choice of medium; the variety and manner of its manipulation; the quality of observation apparent in the visual content and the arrangement and disposition of the various elements in the work. Some of the things the child has done may be intuitive and open to recognition and enjoyment alone; others may support more objective, searching or analytical appraisal. It is through this approach to looking at art that the teacher can introduce painting, drawing, sculpture and other work by artists. Many of the points the teacher would want children to consider are evident in artists' work. For example, the use of colour, the handling of media, the visual content and how it is arranged or simplified and so on. In this way the visual and aesthetic elements of a piece of art can be brought out rather than the purely descriptive or representational ones. Both teacher and children can begin to see that making art is not concerned with merely copying reality but interpreting it. Children can see that there are many different ways of handling visual ideas, and that personal observations and individual approaches to setting down ideas and handling media are as important as getting things to look right.

In other words, the teacher is now in a better and more open position to enable children to understand the visual and aesthetic language of art and how it is used to interpret and communicate meaning. The central dilemma of art, of finding the right form for one's own understanding and visions of what is real, can now be discussed.

The aim should be to make the exchange between teacher and

child, child and children, reciprocal. In this manner the general level of interest and understanding about how each one has seen and portrayed his or her experience will be valued.

It is, perhaps, as much through sharing children's art as any other teaching strategy, that the level of intelligence about visual and aesthetic matters is heightened. I therefore consider some form of sharing through group discussion and conversation, display or annotated exhibition or slide, video, or other visual means, a vital part of teaching art.

To summarise, a possible approach to teaching art is described, bearing in mind that one approach to teaching will catch certain attitudes and ways of working while another will not. The importance of thinking through aims is seen either when they become evident in practice, or the practice becomes so directionless, fragmented and *ad hoc* that it is evident no aims have been considered. Some analysis of the different facets of how children work in art relates directly to the proposed dynamic model of teaching. A number of working principles are set out which arise from the main argument of this and the previous chapter.

Finally, the way that such an approach makes it possible for children to understand what art is about and how to view their own work is seen as an important outcome.

Note

1. Victor D'Amico, *Creative Teaching in Art* (International Textbook Co., 1953), p. 4.

8 PLANNING THE CURRICULUM

Having considered a number of essential aspects of teaching in the last two chapters, it is now time to look at the range of what is taught and how this might be interpreted as an art syllabus. This chapter considers the curriculum range, both in terms of activity and areas of work. It suggests how such a range might be arrived at rather than setting out a definitive or all-inclusive list. The chapter underlines the approach to teaching already discussed and leads into ideas about building a syllabus.

The curriculum is a statement about the various elements which go to make up a course of study. The syllabus is a list, order or sequence of work of various kinds which interprets the curriculum.

The task of planning a curriculum is different from that of setting out a syllabus. In the former, areas of experience and learning are considered in proportion and relationship to each other; in the latter these are interpreted as actual work to be done. Obviously, general statements about curriculum are linked to ideas about the purpose, value and educational worth of doing it — that is to aims.

A curriculum can be interpreted in a wide variety of ways although the underpinning aims would remain the same. The syllabus can be handled in various ways though the work to be covered is more specific. Hence, if drawing was considered to be an element of the curriculum for art education, any kind of drawing would be admissible, whether sketches, diagrams, maps, copies or whatever. In terms of the syllabus, drawing might be specified as the exploration of different media, choice in their use and observation of natural forms. Thus:

Curriculum = the range of experiences considered necessary for the fulfilment of the stated aims for art education
Syllabus = planned sequences or patterns of work

Both of these need to be informed by aims which are likely to change in various ways as experience of art and children making art grows. For example, the following aims could be taken as a way of getting started in planning a curriculum:

(1) To raise children's levels of sensitivity to art materials: what these materials can do and the kinds of images they make.

(2) To heighten children's visual, spatial and tactile awareness of the world around them.

Although we might develop these aims further they are very compatible with the kind of learning children of primary age do and therefore form a satisfactory starting point to indicate the thinking processes behind curriculum planning. It is hoped that these aims will lead to the development of individual work arising from personal discovery as well as direct teaching. They could not, however, lead to the making of artefacts for their own sake as there is a suggestion in the aims that understanding the behaviour of materials and the use of visual observation are essential to the proper fulfilment of these aims. For the children to be expected to place reliance on the teacher's way of seeing and doing things and merely to ape someone else would be a travesty of the aims and art experience.

How does planning a curriculum start? And how does the syllabus develop from this planning? Part of the aim talks about awareness of art materials, but which materials? Over the last few years there has been an enormous increase in the range and variety of materials on offer to schools through catalogues. It is obviously necessary to make some choice between all these different materials and media and specific suggestions are made about this in Chapter 10. To look at the particular range of experiences which different materials offer might be one aspect of the planning. To do this, knowledge and personal experience of making art will help the choice; at whatever level such experience might be, it at least provides a way into the task.

Making marks, drawings, diagrams and so on is one very immediate way of engaging with art materials and their expressive potential. Drawing media are very accessible to children and it would be difficult to imagine art education taking place without some form of drawing. Drawing could, therefore, form one element of the art curriculum which would have to be interpreted in terms of an actual syllabus of work to be followed.

In order to find out something about drawing media, children need to explore them. However, they will have to be helped to do this if such activity is to develop their sensitivity. Such help should not inhibit their enjoyment of the medium and exploration of what it can do, but be watchful for opportunities to encourage personal control of the medium and any ways to heighten awareness of its characteristics. Exploration can reveal the qualities and possibilities of a material or medium: how it behaves, the effects it creates and how it can be controlled. Control of the medium works with its characteristics, organises and relates ideas and impulses to its possible effects. Both exploration and control are essential to raising levels of understanding and awareness, and evidence of this can be seen in the work produced. These comments indicate that consideration of the range of experiences which different materials offer must be linked to the kinds of learning activities that might be anticipated in art.

Apart from encouraging exploration and control of materials, we also need to talk to children about materials and to get them to talk to us about their discoveries. In this way it is possible to focus their attention on the medium and what can be done with it. Such sharing of each other's work increases the range of what is thought possible and builds a vocabulary of words and visual ideas. Looking at the work of artists can form part of the enrichment and extension of this learning. In looking at reproductions or, where possible, the original work of artists, craftsmen, designers and architects, scientists and inventors, it is possible to see drawing used for a whole range of ways of thought and expression. These can be related to the discoveries made by children, providing careful choice of them is made and the children are given ample time to develop confidence to discuss them.

The inventive and expressive ways of using drawing media are then seen to be as valid as the exploratory and observational ones. As the confidence of teacher and children grows, many different ways of handling drawing will emerge, such as explaining maps and models, conceiving inventions and fantasies or expressing ideas and feelings.

From the foregoing it is now possible to deduce a number of activities which are centrally related to any notion of an art curriculum and the experiences different materials might offer.

First, there is the activity of *exploring*. This must be understood as not only exploring media but also ideas which arise through discussion about children's work, how they are helped to look at their own and each other's work: and the work of artists, craftsmen and designers. Notions of exploring will also include those contained in the making of art forms and images such as when working out ideas for painting, print making or sculpture.

Secondly, there is the complementary activity of *ordering* and *controlling*. Here, acquired techniques (whether from school or elsewhere), practised skills, learned methods and developed language will all enable greater autonomy and understanding over the exploratory act. There may be times when the activities of exploring and controlling will continually reinforce each other in close sequence or there could be occasions when practically the whole of a session is dominated by one or the other activity, as when working strongly from an idea or stimulus in a familiar medium.

Thirdly, there are the activities of *sharing* and *appreciating*. These activities focus the attention of the individual on the quality to be found in his own work and that of others. Here the perceptions of visual form (how things look and come to be that way), insights into intention and meaning (what was the artist getting at ? why did he do it that way?) and awareness of cultural and historical context will surface. This is where practice in looking at and discussing art work is important, because it broadens the children's view of what art might be about and particularly because it stimulates memories, associations and relationships from which further ideas, images and actions can arise. Sharing and appreciating in these ways can nourish children's seeing and imagining and give them a broadly based confidence with which to tackle the content/ form tension that inevitably arises in their art work as discussed in Chapter 5.

Fourthly, there are the activities of *inventing* and *expressing*, which arise from personal and novel ways of handling materials and ideas. Exploratory and controlling activities, though essential, are not sufficient to invest the curriculum with individual meaning. This is why exploratory exercises in visual comprehension or just following techniques seldom stimulate personal understanding and endeavour so that it is applied to individual work. There is always the propensity of the human mind to invent and re-combine elements of experience or to be deeply moved and empathise with it. In either case, the activity goes beyond but cannot be without the exploratory, controlling and perceptual activities. However, through invention and imagination the activity of handling materials becomes charged with personal meaning. Such meaning may be fleeting or part of a long, cumulative and persistent tendency to think, feel, imagine or work in particular ways.

I believe that all these activities are essential to the development of the aims where it is the intention of such aims to raise levels of awareness. Furthermore, these four activities are essentially and dynamically related, each enriching and being enriched by the others. Therefore, they must form a central part of the way curriculum is understood.

If we reflect on the way in which children work with materials and our own experience of doing so, it is not difficult to see that these four activities form a natural part of that work. At any age, children will explore materials, try things out, probe them, take them apart and experiment. This is the way in which we can tune in to and re-acquaint ourselves with a material.

Children will devise ways of ordering and controlling materials; impose patterns and games on them and shape them by repetition to their own purposes. They will share and imitate, discuss and criticise, appreciate and applaud.

Lastly, they will do things in their own way, shape them to some imaginative idea or fantasy or, through connections of memory, invent new relationships and forms which arise from deeper associations and give personal meaning to their expression.

Thus, these four activities are an inherent part of the curriculum if part of the aim is to raise levels of awareness and thus take art activity beyond just doing and making from instructions, expectations or stereotypes. All four of these activities — exploring, controlling, appreciating and expressing — in some way or another should be considered when building a curriculum and thereafter planning a syllabus.

We should now return to the experiences which are essentially to do with art in order to see which materials and media can best fulfil aims according to particular circumstances. If the circumstances are such that we have little skill or knowledge, work in a confined space, have limited storage and money, then we must adapt our approach to these limitations. Not to do so could increase frustration, confusion and feelings of inadequacy. To start simply with a carefully chosen, limited range of materials and media could enable organisational and teaching problems to be sorted out more easily. It is much better to build on sound experience of a few materials than sort out the complexities of many, especially where it comes to children's attitudes and expectations.

If circumstances inhibit the craft of pottery, it does not mean that we should abandon any idea of craft work or the provision of clay. It is just that we have to be aware of the limitations and work accordingly.

Perhaps we should start by considering some of the characteristic experiences of art that are likely to be fundamental to art education.

Art is to do with creating and experiencing visual, plastic and three-dimensional images, forms and designs. We use our hands and eyes, or some extension of them, to organise materials into new forms of visual, tactile and spatial experience. This activity may start with copying, describing, observing, analysing and representing, but inevitably involves elements of synthesis, adaptation, invention and so on, which arise from memory, imagination and the response to stimuli and the power to reconstruct and visualise.

All this sounds very complex and probably cannot help to plan a curriculum, so there is a need to get at the planning in a simpler way — perhaps by considering the actual experiences available in particular types of material. The two-dimensional (flat — as on paper) visual experience of drawing is probably the simplest to conceive. With young children, this involves the accumulation of a repertoire or language of marks, similar to the language of words. On the basis of this mark-making language children develop the capacity to describe, annotate and invent from the world around them. Through drawing they can convey a host of things about their experience of the world which are not easily conveyed by verbal language. Shape, size, proportion, relationship, scale, surface, texture and rhythm are all expressed more readily through making marks than using words. Therefore, drawing seems an essential experience to be included in the art curriculum.

It is possible to conceive of various types of drawing according to the intention or motivation of the artist and this is considered in Chapter 11 where assessment and evaluation are discussed. Intention and motivation are also important factors to consider when looking at the use of other materials.

Another area of visual experience is that to do with colour. There are many media which enable children to work with colour, such as pencil crayons, printing inks, threads and coloured papers. However, the most accessible and powerful agent for experiencing colour in all its range and subtlety is surely paint. The fluidity, texture, transparency, vibrancy and impasto characteristics of paint make it an essential experience in the art curriculum. It also allows simple forms of print and pattern making and, with different additives, is widely applicable to other uses.

Both drawing and painting are two-dimensional, most usually being applied to a flat surface. Therefore, it seems important that some three-dimensional experience should be available in the art curriculum which enables children to be involved in form and space. Once again there is a considerable range from which to choose. For example, card, wood, plasticine, clay, papier maché and plaster. However, we have to consider which material can provide the greatest versatility with the least problems. At first sight card may seem simple and plentifully available from second-hand sources, yet it is limited in the way it can be handled, requires some tools and produces a narrow range of forms. Plasticine seems another possible choice, but this is expensive for the amount we can afford and softens as it is used. Both these things limit its use to small items only. Clay seems to offer the richest possibilities for three-dimensional experience. It is plastic and malleable and, as it dries out on exposure to air and through handling, it becomes more rigid. It is an extremely flexible medium and can be used in a liquid state as slip, soft and malleable to make forms and solids, and in a leather-hard state from which to build and construct. It is not always necessary to fire clay but if this means of making it more permanent is available, it can be used. In my view, clay provides another essential experience, where form, space and solidity can all be experienced in expressive and constructional ways.

These materials might be extended to include some form of print making and work with fabric and thread. Print making introduces a range of new experiences to do with the repetion, amalgamation, overlaying and combining of shapes and colours. Sometimes these will be used for single images with a limited edition, at other times for a repeated or assembled pattern. Fabric is familiar to all of us in clothes and furnishings, yet how few children have the chance to really explore it and use it as a creative medium. The richness in colour and texture in its composition and structure all lend themselves to a variety of experiences. Fabric can be added to by stitching, dyeing and collage and is very versatile. It seems to me that some form of print making and work with fabric and thread should be included in the art curriculum.

There are other materials which provide unique areas of experience, such as those to do with sculpture or photography, but these cannot be considered to be as basic to the art curriculum for five- to thirteen-year-old children as those already mentioned, even though there will be schools that cater for these experiences. We have now reached the point where we can add to our art-curriculum thinking the range of materials, each one of which provides the possibility for specific kinds of art experience.

Hence it would seem necessary to provide the following basic range of types of media if the aims are to be fulfilled: (1) drawing media, (2) paint, and (3) clay. To these, then, might be added: (4) print-making materials and (5) fabric and thread. Other media and materials may be chosen for personal reasons such as the enthusiasm or peculiar knowledge of the teacher.

I should also mention found, waste and scrap materials which are used in abundance by some schools. In my view there are a number of problems peculiar to this range of materials, which are described in Chapter 10. However, they can add to and supplement the work of drawing, painting and three-dimensional work, if selected and used with care, but are in themselves no substitute for the range stated, nor should they supplant any of them. However, their possible use in constructions and inventions should be mentioned.

Construction and Invention

Children enjoy exploring objects, fitting them together and trying out different experiences with them. This is particularly so after the age of seven when their interest in how things function and fit together, or can be made to work, develops strongly. Many children enjoy experimenting with objects and materials, taking them apart and inventing new things with them. Children enjoy making camps and houses, creating personal collections and environments in their bedrooms or playspaces, using objects to play out in fantasy many of the things they see in the adult world around them.

In order to sustain fantasy play, an object may have to look real, have specific details or parts of it actually work. This is especially so where other children are going to share the play and the object that stimulates or sustains it. But the need for the object to share and sustain play creates problems to be sorted out. In the process of finding or devising solutions to such problems children will become very inventive using and adapting objects and materials to all kinds of play purposes.

This inventiveness is a strong source of motivation in children's learning and can promote the use of a variety of materials other than paint, clay and graphic media, such as wood, and metal in the forms of thin strip and sheet and plastic, also constructional toys like Lego and Meccano. In all this making and inventing children's own ideas are of paramount importance as the source of motivation and confidence; therefore they should have their ideas listened to and respected even though these may not appear capable of realisation. This point is brought out strongly in *Children's Growth through Creative Experience.*[1]

Inventiveness and an interest in construction and making lead naturally to planning, thinking about and designing. Many children enjoy this aspect of handling materials and seem especially affected by the solidity and presence, the spatial and functional aspects of the objects which result. It is not easy for them to move from a two-dimensional, abstract concept, to a three-dimensional, solid object, and much of their designing and inventing is through playing about with and trying out ideas with materials directly rather than thinking on paper. The ideas of Edward de Bono show us the enormous potential of children in this respect, as do many of the approaches and attitudes to learning to be found in *Science 5 - 13*[2] and the work and ideas of the Design Education movement.

Lastly, but by no means least, attention should be drawn to craftwork as such, not for the traditional practices alone, but particularly for the attitudes and experiences which it embodies which can be so satisfying and significant for children. Traditionally, craftwork has been associated with natural materials which occur in specific localities or regions and have been used in many functional, decorative and symbolic ways as part of the traditions of the communities which use them.

Methods for treating, preparing and forming such materials as cane, straw, wood, wool, fibres and natural dyestuffs have been evolved over generations. Therefore the practice of a craft can embody much more than the physical acts of making and, when it is shared with older members of the community, can be something magical and very special for children.

The pleasure derived from finding and collecting materials for craftwork is considerable, particularly for junior-age children who have a natural inclination to collect and hoard. Craft materials almost dictate certain kinds of approaches in which care becomes important and the methodical accumulation, building up, or transformation of material, becomes a measured and absorbing activity.

Often there is a specific end in view towards which the work proceeds. The item produced is most often valued for its decorative, functional or symbolic content without the need to ascribe to it personal or expressive meaning. The forms produced will reflect the methods of preparation and making as much as the idiosyncracy of the maker.

Craftwork in schools can too easily be subordinated to learning and practising a craft skill; therefore the teacher needs to handle the teaching of technique with sensitivity so that children acquire sufficient knowledge to be able to work with a material, yet retain some flexibility to handle it in their own way. The rhythms and sequences, the resistances and patterns through which objects are formed from materials are as much felt through the fingers and the body as conceived and known about in the mind. It is this intuitive feeling for rightness and empathy that can be so satisfying when working in a craft.[3]

Looking and Seeing

The next part of the aim to be embodied in the curriculum is that concerned with looking, whether this is looking at the world around us, the products of our own endeavours, or those of others. Clearly, one way in which the teacher can help children to develop their powers of perception is through the children's own experience of making art. Children need to be helped to see in their art more than its ability to represent the world of object, for art has its visual and aesthetic dimension at whatever level this exists. Visual and aesthetic qualities are different from those which arise from direct copies or representations of the actual world although they may be similar, for each person will see and experience the world differently and these differences will be manifest in visual and aesthetic qualities such as the arrangement of shapes and kind of colour used. If we do nothing to help children to be perceptive and informed in their looking they will have only a limited means of response which is likely to be guided by the visually most articulate (but not necessarily most perceptive or sensitive) members of the group. Furthermore, they will be prey to the current stereotypes which they, and often the teacher, unthinkingly accept.

So where do we start with looking? Of course there are all kinds of starting places, but I will take two. First, the looking which is involved in exploring a medium. At first sight the suggestion to explore a medium (say in drawing) might seem to be an invitation to scribble. Scribble can involve many of the elements of more sophisticated and controlled drawing if the scribbler is alerted to the effects and action of scribbling. Change in rhythm, pace, extension and pressure of the fingers and the direction of the medium can all increase the range and quality of a scribbled line. Thus, when a given group of children has produced its first exploratory drawings (say after five minutes) it is necessary for the teacher to look at the results with them. Through a series of questions, comments, observations and directions, the teacher and children can together begin to extend the notion of exploration. Areas of lines, thick and thin, dense and packed on top of each other (producing darker tones), shapes and in-fills, textures and patterns, all become evident as ways of seeing and extending the first exploratory scribbles.

We then have to look for elements of control in the way different children organise and develop their explorations. At this point other kinds of looking can become relevant, such as looking at drawings by artists which show similar ways of exploring surfaces and textures, shapes and tones. Thus, a collection of reproductions, acquired from books, colour supplements, catalogues and exhibitions can be as important a resource as objects to look at. The way in which children develop the capacity to focus on aspects of their drawings can be directly transferred to drawings by artists and become a natural way into widening their understanding.

Young children, pre-seven-year-olds, will not make comparisons, search for similarities or make connections in the way that post-seven-year-olds will. This is because they are not yet able to build concepts independently from their experience. However, they can enjoy looking at artists' work and may imitate it through the use of their own vocabulary of marks or schema. Perhaps the experience goes in through the pores as a feeling and knowing extension of how they see the world from their egocentric standpoint.

The other 'looking' resource is obviously the range and variety of actual objects which are available in the classroom. These should be as varied as possible but can, at the outset, be acquired directly and cheaply from local sources. Natural forms (stones, bones, wood pieces, roots, branch forms, dried plants and skeleton leaves, feathers, stalks, growing plants and flowers, leaf buds and so on), scrap items (parts of cars, machines, dynamos, telephones, scrap metal). We should be very selective, and should definitely clean items of excess dirt and oil and keep and present them with care. Looking is focused both by choice and presentation. A piece of rusty iron in a display of browns or related to textured surfaces can become a jewel. Historical, cultural and personal interest items can also be displayed. Some of these can be valuable or fragile yet the aim should be to help children to develop the sensitivity to handle them. The qualities of light through glass can be magical, so bottles, glasses, prisms, stoppers and tubes might all be acquired over a period of time. Items such as cane work, ceramics, macramé and fabrics, which may be acquired for personal pleasure, can also be shared with children. There has been a vogue for Victoriana, which has evoked and excited responses to that period through handling actual objects more than any amount of words could do. Items from more recent times can also have this quality and are more readily available from flea markets and junk shops. There are also objects from other cultures and parts of the world which are becoming more plentiful in shops. All of these sources of looking, as well as local museums, houses, galleries, craft shops and fac-tories, should be drawn into the repertoire of visual resources at the disposal of the teacher.

One of the problems with looking is that it often remains super-ficial and unfocused. We could say that looking is different from seeing. The former is an outward moving activity which enables us to find our way through the maze of experiences and sensations around us to achieve specific ends that are often nothing to do with looking. For example, when we go shopping we have a specific end in view and use looking to achieve it. In the process, we may never see a friend, or a change in the environment that was not there previously. Seeing, on the other hand, is more focused and inward; attention is arrested and we are likely to be affected by what we see and even changed by it. Therefore, it is important to find ways of helping children to see and much of the teaching in art must be directed towards increasing children's visual awareness.[4]

Art objects concentrate seeing in very special and peculiar ways. It is not the object, person or view, as such, which is important but the way in which it is seen and the particular associations, memo-ries, emotions and responses it evokes — in other words, its parti-cular embodiment of meaning. Meaning, in this sense, will also be culturally contexted, so that the kinds of associations and relationships which find their way into visual appearances and forms will be of their culture and period in history. Beyond, yet part of this, will be the symbol and image quality of the work. This particular quality of a work of art is hard to define but has the effect of changing our awareness and consciousness of ourselves in relation to our experience: we both see and feel things differently because of the power of images. When children look at the work of artists, they respond to these aspects of the work but in ways that grow from their understanding and vocabulary. Thus, a question or observation about a particular shape or colour may not have a direct answer or need any comment for it is sufficient that the experience has registered on the awareness of the child. Clearly, the kind of extensions to a child's understanding and view of art can grow immeasurably through sharing in the work of artists. This aspect of learning must also find its place in the art curriculum, where the inventions, expression and direct response of a child to some experience or stimulus both evokes and is triggered by a deeper sense of meaning, knowing and participation, than mere appearance or association of objects.

Thus, the range of materials used in making art and the visual and aesthetic experiences which they engender lie at the centre of curriculum planning and are the means whereby the aims for art education are interpreted. The activities of exploring and controlling media and expressing and sharing art images and forms are the actions by which children's education in art is enriched and extended.

To summarise, following the distinction between curriculum and syllabus, the planning of a curriculum is discussed, based on the stated aims for art education. Exploration and control are cited as basic activities in achieving the curriculum aims to which are added sharing and appreciating and inventing and expressing. In the light of these four areas of activity, a range of areas of work is suggested without which a curriculum for art would not make sense. Hence:

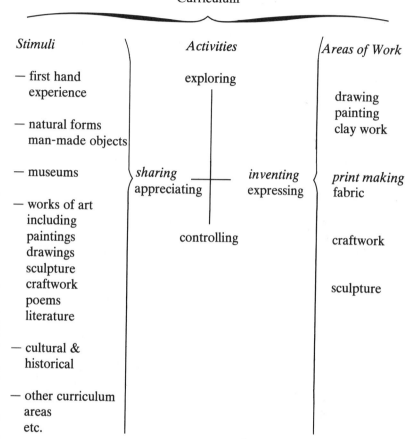

Aims for an
Art Education
Curriculum

Stimuli

— first hand
  experience

— natural forms
  man-made objects

— museums

— works of art
  including
  paintings
  drawings
  sculpture
  craftwork
  poems
  literature

— cultural &
  historical

— other curriculum
  areas
  etc.

Activities

exploring

sharing ———— *inventing*
appreciating   expressing

controlling

Areas of Work

drawing
painting
clay work

print making
fabric

craftwork

sculpture

Notes

1. Schools Council Art and Craft Project 8-13 (Van Nostrand Reinhold, 1973).
2. Schools Council.
3. See Seonaid Robertson, *Creative Crafts in Education* (Routledge and Kegan Paul, 1952), p. 4.
4. See Victor D'Amico, *Creative Teaching in Art* (International Textbook Co., 1953), p. 9.

9 BUILDING A SYLLABUS

Having thought the way through one approach to planning a curriculum, it is now appropriate to consider how the results of this thinking find substance and expression through the building of a syllabus. To this end I will take a number of examples and work them through, as if with children, in the hope that the underlying principles will become evident, despite the assumptions that will have to be made about children's responses.

Presumably one's aims are not abandoned when thinking about the kind of things one wants children to do, both in what they may learn and in the work they may produce. Even if aims are neither written down nor clearly identified (both of which help the teacher to become more effective, in my view) they will surely surface in what is done, how it is approached and in the way any outcomes are managed by the teacher.

Therefore, underlying these examples will be the following objectives derived from the broad statement of aims set out in Chapters 7 and 8.

(1) To stimulate and heighten children's perception of visual, tactile and spatial qualities in their own work and that of others, including that of artists, craftmen and designers. Through discussion, questions and other forms of shared looking and responding, to develop a critical awareness of visual, aesthetic and design qualities.

(2) To develop children's capacity to explore and control media and through this to communicate ideas and responses visually and spatially.

(3) To develop practical and critical skills.

(4) To learn, devise, invent and apply techniques and to acquire knowledge about art and design.

(5) To establish simple routines for handling the medium which children will be encouraged to adopt whenever they wish to work in a two or three dimensional way with visual media.

Paint

For this example the chosen medium is powder colour and, before any session in which it is to be used, some preparation is necessary. The range of colours made available should be decided on. Powder colour can be awkward to handle unless resonably well contained in small pots, which are best placed on trays. Too many colours can increase problems of storage and dispensing; too few can limit the range of discoveries. Generally speaking it seems wiser to add to a palette of colours as children's confidence and enjoyment in mixing grows. More specific notes about paints are to be found in Chapter 10.

Colours should always be clean and dry and one palette should be provided between two children if possible. Mixing trays, water pots, small and medium brushes should be provided, and small pieces of paper, black, white and grey. Provision to change the water fairly often should be made. Clean newspaper on which to paint and if possible a small rag or sponge — one between two — on which to blot over-full brushes, is also useful. These are the basic requirements.

Other items which the teacher can have to hand as means to develop or extend some of the likely discoveries the children may make are as follows:

To manipulate the paint: strips of card, sticks, spatulas, paste-spreaders, palette knives etc.

To add to the paint texture: paste, fine sand, tissue paper, PVA adhesive etc.

To extend the paint surface: small blocks of wood, pieces of sponge, card shapes, string etc.

These extra items may not be called upon but can be available as part of the teacher's resources to enable him to respond to the children's discoveries in a variety of ways. As well as these items, he should have other resources to encourage looking, such as coloured or patterned stones and shells, textured and patterned feathers, leaves and plants, pieces of wood and bark and so on. Finally, he should have to hand examples of paintings and details of painted surfaces to share and compare with the children's work. These can be culled from colour supplements, postcards, exhibition catalogues, second-hand books, or use can be made of books and actual paintings.

Perhaps none of the above items will be used, but on the other hand, they could form a vital and important part in extending the work of the children and raising their level of awareness and intelligence about paint. It could arise that without such planning of back-up resources, the teacher is left with no means of shifting the direction, emphasis, or development of the work and could find himself forced back into ways of working and responding that are inappropriate to the above aims. For example, his response to children's painting may be limited to subjective comments and personal preferences instead of a more open dialogue which could enlarge the children's attitude to art.

The teacher's experience of children will also be part of his preparation. He will be able to assume that some parts of the work will be accomplished quickly and others will require more insistence on taking care and real looking, or specific direction.

Starting Session

Let us assume that the teacher is going to work with the whole group, though this is not always best, and that the room with the materials is set out with care.

The teacher attempts to get the children thinking about powder paint and handling it with some focusing of their attention. He knows they will have met powder colour before and most of them will have an attitude towards it. However, he considers that it is important to stimulate their perceptions about how paint behaves and the range of experience possible.

After the first exchange of questions and answers about it, the children are asked to explore the medium in its dry state on grey or white paper. As soon as the children start, it is important for the teacher to observe the different ways in which children behave with the paint. This is where good preparation counts, for the children will have all they need for work without taking the teacher's attention away from his observations of the class. Some will ask more questions of the teacher, or of each other; they do not really know what is expected of them. Some will do what they have always done, others will copy them. Others will enjoy the medium, feeling, spreading and mixing it on the paper. Giving them a small piece of paper (not bigger than A5) resting on newspaper will help them contain their explorations.

Soon the changed level of sound, the lessening of concentration and so on, will indicate that it is necessary to stop the session in order to look at the outcomes with the children and bring back into focus the point of what they are doing. This is the time when it becomes possible to evolve and share a verbal and visual language with the children leading to some critical awareness of paint qualities because they have now produced examples from which to work. The qualities of softness, intermixing, brilliance and so forth can be brought out, as can the care and consideration, or otherwise, with which the exploration has been pursued. What is meant by exploration, and the kind of activities which are associated with it, should now become more evident to the children.

Further explorations could now take place on the black paper which will show up the colour differently, or the idea of mixing with water could be introduced, depending on how well the teacher feels the children understand what they are doing and the level of their practical and critical skills. The teacher has various options on how he initiates the mixing of paint and water. These range from allowing the children to explore it in an open and free way, to demonstrating to them the starting procedures to be followed. No one way is right; the important point is that whatever is done aims to increase the confidence, care and understanding of the children about the way they handle the powder colour. Their own invention and application of technique is valid and can be discussed in the context of the whole experience.

Later, when the children explore, they should have a much clearer idea of what is entailed and understand the teacher is looking for the different ways in which paint is mixed and applied to the surface of the papers. The teacher can observe what discoveries the children make which may add to or develop the way he talks to them. Thus the paint may be mixed thickly or thinly on the palette or the paper, run together, or be painted over, applied in single strokes, and spots, or flat areas and so on.

The noise level will subside as the children's attention is drawn back into their work and their energy becomes more focused on the way the material behaves. The teacher's observations will show him when some children over-work an idea, do not keep brush and water clean, need to stop and reflect or are captivated by some quality in their work. All of these kinds of observation are important for the contribution they can make to sharing the work later.

It is now much more likely that the children will be more forthcoming about the discoveries they have made and more perceptive when looking at what other children have done because their own experience, as found in the work, is used to help them. The teacher will be able to see evidence of different ways of manipulating the paint and attempts by the children to organise and control it. The teacher must attempt to help the children see the various qualities and enjoy the effects of paint, whether these are to do with tactile qualities such as softness of blending, transparent wateriness, or thicker impasto overlays, or colour qualities such as softness of hues, clash or contrast of kinds of colour, or blends and atmospheric qualities. There will be various ways which the children have used to organise the paint so that it does not remain a series of formless patches and marks for example, making patterns, repeating shapes, creating outlines of objects or letters, folding the paper on the paint or making the explorations into actual pictures. Such things are evidence of the children looking for ways to control the paint and give it form.

All of these things can and will be noticed by the children and lead to other observations and possibilities. The teacher may wish to introduce objects to look at which are simple to paint yet have exciting colour, pattern or texture. These would introduce another aspect of careful looking and function as a control on the way the children handle the medium. It may be that additional mixing with the paint, to help children get a better consistency, would be right. Set out below are some of the possible developments, depending on how the children have managed the kind of responses and ideas coming from them.

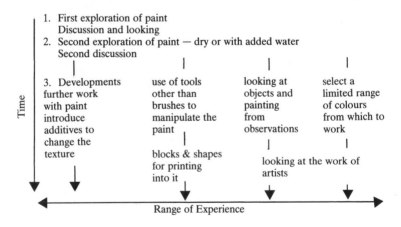

It can now be seen that from the teacher's observations of the children and from discussing and sharing their work with them, a number of possible developments will arise, any one of which could be worth pursuing. In those suggested above, futher work in texture and surface, in printing and printed surfaces, in looking and painted approximations, or in colour and colour observations could be developed.

It might be that the children would be sufficiently familiar with the organisation of the room and materials to work in a number of small groups and the teacher, having planned ahead for the session, could produce stimuli appropriate to each area. Children's ideas and what they see in the work is obviously important and, together with the teacher's experience, can accomplish futher work with paint.

Through all these developments the teacher will watch and hope for signs of growing confidence in the children to make choices, attempt innovations, practice and extend skills, develop their own techniques, and show in their work personal observations, awareness of colour qualities and sensitivity to the forms and images of paint. He will hope that as many children as possible will enjoy using paint as one of the media with which they choose to interpret and communicate their ideas and observations.

Paint, as one element in the curriculum, could be interpreted in syllabus terms as in the following example.

Paint (a) powder colour. Different kinds of exploratory work leading to:

colour mixing from restricted palette	mixing additives textural qualities	colour qualities and strengths areas and overlays
colour from observation of objects, town/landscape	observation of surfaces and textures	of colour transparency
stimulated by happenings, stories, events, poems	printed shapes and textures	use of shapes to extend painted areas
looking at and discussing paintings	painting from objects with a variety of tools	shape and colour print making

The first few sessions could begin with different kinds of exploration of the medium leading towards smaller groups or individuals working in different ways.

Thus, the use of paint as part of the syllabus can develop in a variety of ways and once the work with children has enabled this to happen, these ways will always be available to the teacher for further extension. Each group of children will make something different of the same initial experience or stimulus and, in this way, keep the work dynamic and developing. It should be possible to take any of the curriculum areas and use the same kind of principles to develop a syllabus unit from them. Of course, aims can be interpreted in a variety of ways, so that we should now consider another example, but rather differently, in order to bring out the principle that a syllabus develops with the children not despite them.

Print Making

The next example of syllabus building concerns print making but, this time, several stages on, so it can be assumed that children are used to handling and mixing colours. Although the first session could be with powder colour mixed with a small quantity of water paste or liquid soap to stop it drying out, the use of water-soluble printing inks will be assumed for this example. Wherever it is possible it is worth budgeting for the best quality materials one can afford. This is another reason for restricting the range of materials used. Printing inks are finely ground and mix easily as well as having the right consistency to achieve good printed surfaces, therefore there is considerable advantage in using them. Please see Chapter 10 for more details on materials.

Careful preparation is necessary, whether working with a small or large group, so that the right attitude towards handling the processes of print making are adopted. Apart from the colour range of printing inks, the following are essential: newspaper to cover surfaces, to act as a pad on which to print and to be used to clean up; clean water and a rag or sponge, one between two children; a large brush and palette knife each, a mixing spatula or paste spreader, one between two; a flat sheet of metal or perspex or thick glass on which to mix the ink, one between two; and, if possible, a roller. A useful addition is a soft pad made from sponge or old tights wrapped in plastic and covered with cotton cloth. This can be used to transfer printing ink to any surface. To start with, small pieces of clean newsprint are needed on which experiments can be made.

Print making has much to do with surfaces, textures and patterns, therefore various means are found to introduce children to surfaces and focus their looking and touching on them. The ways in which colours and shapes interact and overlay each other as surfaces are built up is also a characteristic and exciting feature of printed surfaces. These visual qualities of printed surfaces are not readily understood or appreciated by children, who will sometimes paint them in where they do not register.

Another part of the preparation, therefore, is to collect scraps of materials and different surfaces from which prints can be made. These can be placed in (shoe) boxes on each table for possible use as the session develops. The kind of things to collect include small blocks and surfaces of wood, cotton reels, pieces of plastic, bottle tops, corks, nuts and bolts, large screws, pieces of fabric such as net or hessian, paper from wallpaper books or wrappings, corrugated and plain card. Any item, having a broken surface or shape, which can be held easily in the hand or managed on a table-top can be used. Through experience, selection and choice will give this range variety without it being cumbersome or difficult to handle.

Bearing in mind the overall curriculum aims, set out at the beginning of the chapter the cluster of aims for print making should include the following:

(1) To encourage children to recognise, understand and enjoy the characteristics and special qualities of printed surfaces, both their own and others — including those of practising artists.

(2) To help children to see possibilities for interpreting and developing their observations and ideas in terms of printed images and designs.

(3) To promote in children a methodical, craftsmanlike approach to processes of print making — which they are shown, or evolve for themselves — and to encourage them to develop a respect for materials.

Starting Session

A range of objects, both natural forms and man-made items, are brought into the room to display and share with children, who are given time to look at and handle objects before the teacher discusses them. This range of objects could include some of the following: pieces of wood and bark, leafy and twiggy plants, items of clothing (footwear, hats, shawls), fruits and vegetables, all selected for their quality of surface and colour, rusty or part-painted metal, old utensils or tools, machine parts, implements — any items which have interest in their texture, pattern, shape or colour. Stuffed birds and animals and other such items,often available from museums or local authority collections, form a range of stimuli from which children can choose and to which they are drawn.

The session proceeds with the teacher really focusing the looking and attention of the group on the surface qualities of the objects, such as contrasts in appearance and touch. He encourages the children to bring out in discussion similarities and differences, to investigate and analyse the surfaces to see whether they are part of the structure, applied to the surface, or arising from a pattern of growth.

Next, he reminds them about what they have done, and what they know of exploring a material or medium. They look at the printing ink together and certain points are made about handling it with care, achieving the right consistency and mixing. It is easier to modify light and weak colours by mixing small quantities of dark or strong colour into them than the other way round. The children are also asked to experiment with small blocks of wood and pieces of card in order to obtain some kind of printed surface. The making of prints from simple surfaces is one easy way of finding out about printing and the qualities that can be achieved.

If the majority of the group appears keen to try, and seem to understand what is expected of them, the exploration can start. If there appears considerable doubt, further explanation may be necessary, or even a simple demonstration. An introduction of more than fifteen to twenty minutes is often too long for children to listen to the teacher talking about the work and his observations for they need to get into the experience in order to understand it and develop ideas.

It is important for the teacher to observe the patterns of work that now follow. These patterns will be as varied as any group of children and reveal some who do not yet understand what to do, others who want to talk more about the stimulus and follow someone else's lead, others who enjoy paint and colour and immediately start handling the medium and others who spend time plotting out what to do. The teacher recognises that there are different ways of getting started and that these encompass the four areas of perception, response, skill and technique. Some children want to go on talking about and looking at the objects; others want to get their fingers into the printing ink; others seem to have an idea which they want to try out and yet others want to know what they should do. In other words, the dynamic process described in Chapter 6 has started and will continue to develop as long as the teacher has confidence and does not impose arbitrary goals or results on the activity.

The teacher knows that the range of experience taking place across the whole group is most valuable for the teaching material and real experience it provides. As soon as the first wave of activity begins to subside or fragment, the work is stopped and, by various means, the teacher should attempt to focus the attention of the children on any surface/print qualities which have been produced. These will group in various ways and include, for example, direct pattern making using the shapes printed, individual and random prints using as many different objects as possible, and heavily painted surfaces where the ink has been too thick. Any of the work can be used for discussion about the qualities and problems to be found in print making. Some children may have consciously started to organise the printed marks into pictures or balanced designs.

During the discussion about the prints which children have produced, the teacher can emphasise certain points which he feels are vital to an understanding of print making. Such things as the consistency of the ink, the arrangement and care of the working space and the choice of surfaces and colours are essential to good printmaking and can be reinforced when discussing the children's work. Later on these exchanges will enable the teacher to talk about printed images and the particular qualities these can have.

As children enter puberty, the image content can become more significant to them yet be frustrated by their demands for detail or exactness. Print making offers them a way of resolving this conflict (the content/form tension described in Chapter 5) by producing print images rather than striving for realistic copies. Thus, the kind of discussions which become possible with children after the age of seven have an important bearing on later understanding.

From this moment there are a number of possible routes to further work, each one valid in the context of the response of the children so far and the purposes of the teacher. A specific task could be set whereby they are asked to interpret a textured object in terms of the shapes and surfaces they have available. Or again, the colours and a limited range of shapes could be suggested for the development of a built-up, tessalated or overlaid pattern surface. Arising from the way children have looked at and discussed their experiments, there could be a number of imaginative ideas which they want to pursue. One can select parts of objects by masking or magnifying them and use these as a way of starting a print. Cutting stencils, shapes and masks and using them to block out print on to a surface could be another development.

Each idea for extending the work with surfaces, textures, shapes and colours, should explore the ways in which children's awareness to printed surfaces can become more perceptive and therefore intelligent.

Thus the first explorations with print making can lead to various other developments in the syllabus and extend the range of work and understanding available to the teacher.

Print Making
    Looking at textured and patterned objects
    Discussion
    Experimental work
    Discussion

A	B	C
drawing all or part of an object	experiments with small blocks of wood and printing ink (one colour)	mixing colours by spreading and rolling printing ink
simplifying shapes on paper or card and using them as printing surfaces	building up surfaces with black/white and one colour to interpret the textures of objects	use of shapes for printing, arrangement of coloured areas: experiments in colour overlay and juxtaposition
building up surfaces on a rectangle of card using fabric, card, textured paper, strong etc. to make a block from which to make wax rubbings and prints	textured surfaces and materials to build up paintings	stencils, cut shapes and masks, derived from looking at the environment

A   This line of development is concerned with the tactile quality of surfaces where the finger tips come into contact with different surfaces in the process of building them up, making a rubbing and pulling a print from the surface of the block.

B   This development works towards the awareness of the appearance of different surfaces. The restriction on the colours used heightens the effect of texture and pattern which can be related to looking for similar surfaces in the environment and developing paintings from such observations.

C   This development can bring into focus the quality of shape and colour in print making — how these two things interact and overlay each other. All kinds of observations can be made which show these qualities, such as those from reflections in glass and water, transparency in plants and skies and juxtapositions in building colours and patterns.

There are obviously other approaches and lines of development apart from those set out here. The ones I have chosen to describe indicate how it is possible for one idea to grow from another, one line of thinking or experience to promote futher work, and for one's aims to be interpreted in a variety of ways.

This approach develops the syllabus in such a way that it need not deny getting ideas and methods from other teachers or books and magazines, providing they are used with sensitivity to the children's needs and the furtherance of one's educational aims. I believe it to be necessary for the lines of development of the syllabus to arise from the work which children do, and how they do it, as much as from the teacher's knowledge of methods and his expectation of certain kinds of results. It is the blending of the teacher's experience and knowledge with the child's own ideas, responses and abilities which enables understanding to grow. There is something reciprocal in the way the teacher accepts the discoveries and understandings of a child and is prepared to shape his thinking about the syllabus to the appropriate development of the child's learning. If the teacher has set methods which he expects followed and wants specific kinds of results which he already sees in his mind's eye, the dynamic development of the syllabus will be curbed and even dry up, to be gradually replaced by the supermarket or tasty-snack syllabus in which things to do are taken randomly from any available source and given to children to keep them amused or busy. It is then that the search for what to do next starts.

There is little real educational point in children producing prints by labouring through mechanical processes to satisfy the teacher's expectations. The real purposes of the art education are too important to be lost in such practices. Underlying all the methods shown and techniques taught, is the need for every child to grow in confidence to use visual ideas and respond to experience through images of one sort or another. At the heart of everything produced must be the growing awareness in children of the forms and images in the whole world around them. Their increased sensitivity to visual images and the sources of ideas, feelings and imagination in their own experience will enable them to interpret the world and thus make it hold more personal meaning.

Print making has the potential to do all these things if the teacher can trust himself and the children he teaches. Such trust leads to heightened perception of the way children work and the art they produce. It does this precisely because there are no firm and positive answers to making art. Where dogmatism creeps in, sensitivity becomes abandoned. There is a subtle balance between what the child knows and can do and how he responds or has the confidence to follow intuitions. Whether this colour or that is right will depend partly on the child's understanding of how to arrive at changes of colour and partly as an instinct to know when he has the right one. Of course, there will be problems of drawing and detail, but these should not be allowed to dominate other aspects of art form such as relationships of shape, contrasts or harmonies of colour, qualities of surface and so on.

Both children and teacher will only come to a deeper and richer understanding of printed images by sustained experience and continually returning to the medium, rather than engaging in one-off novelty sessions, and this is so for any art medium.

Clay

I feel that it might be helpful if I now consider one more example of syllabus building taking a three-dimensional material such as clay. The merits of clay as a material have already been described in Chapter 8. It is plastic — that is, it can be pushed and pulled to take any shape; it is three-dimensional — it occupies space and is solid; it is expressive, responding readily to the touch of the fingers. Clay can accept and retain the least or greatest impressions in its form or on its surface; and it can be a constructional material, one can build up and add to its forms in various ways.

There are certain characteristics of clay which are vital for children to understand. First when it is exposed to air or handled, it continuously dries out, which means that it gets harder and more rigid. Secondly, clay behaves strangely with water, being impervious to it yet forming a thick, sticky slurry when mixed with water. Completely dried clay will crumble and break down into this slurry when placed in water, yet partly dried clay will become lumpy and unmanageable if wet. Thirdly, when clay is subjected to high temperatures, in a fire or a kiln, its chemical nature changes and it becomes one of the most enduring and decay-resistant materials. (See Figure 9.1, p.163.)

Bearing these points in mind, much of the early work with clay will have to be concerned with helping children to understand its nature. If children have experienced clay at an earlier stage much of the preliminary exploratory work will be unnecessary, though it is often valuable to have some time handling clay before committing oneself to a particular idea. Therefore, this session assumes some experience of the material and is informed by the following aims:

(1) To encourage children to handle their ideas with awareness and understanding of the characteristics of clay.

(2) To enlarge their understanding of the different forms in which clay can be used to interpret ideas and responses. Their confidence to make their own images is to be supported by looking at the work of others, including artists and craftsmen where appropriate.

(3) To develop a workmanlike approach to the preparation, care and handling of clay, whether this involves firing and glazing or not. To think about the forms they want to make and how best to achieve them, whether by inventing and evolving techniques, or following accepted practices in their planning.

Preparation

Usually clay is supplied to schools in plastic bags. If these are sound and have no splits or tears, which allow air to dry the clay

Figure 9.1: Angel

Clay is malleable and plastic and can be shaped and formed easily. It is three-dimensional in that it can occupy space and be built up. It is also expressive in that it takes the least impression and keeps it.

out, the material should keep in working condition for a long time. Bags should be opened carefully so that they can be tightly sealed to exclude any air.

Other items which may be required include large brushes, hessian covered boards on which to work (hardboard would do), an assortment of wooden tools (these can be shaped from bamboo cane), old kitchen knives, rolling pins, newspaper and a box of assorted shapes and objects which can be pressed into clay to form textures and patterns. In primary school one would usually work with a small group — say, not more than ten children — while the others were busy with something else. In middle or secondary school, larger groups may be encountered but the more specialist provision would, to some extent, help make this possible.

For the stimulus to this session, the groups might have been out drawing parts of buildings, noticing particularly the surfaces and textures, patterns and types of material used and the way parts of the building are joined and supported. These records of their observations are to be used as a starting point for a piece of clay-work. The initial experiments with the medium (clay) are designed to tune the children in to its possibilities and stimulate ideas about how it might be used to interpret their observations and ideas.

The children are asked to work in an exploratory way with the material which is presented to them in a small ball. What does it mean to explore? They could be asked this question, or it could form the basis for a short discussion. You want them to explore its properties and qualities but go beyond this to conceive experiments with the materials relating to their ideas. The first explorations could include pinching, prodding, flattening and rolling, piling up and pulling apart. The relative elasticity and moulding properties will be felt and the weight, temperature and solidity of the clay experienced. Children who have not experienced clay before will, more likely, finish up with a pile of little bits, some already drying out. If they have had some experience this will be evident in the kinds of changes made in the clay and how these are kept together. Once again it would be necessary to look at the work done and to talk about it, sharing discoveries and possibilities across the group and generating futher ideas. Evidence of children trying to control the material could be discussed as ways of interpreting ideas. Such control will take various forms such as imposing ideas on the material which may or may not be appropriate, making patterns or shapes with it and so on. If clay is worked on a board there is a strong tendency for it to get flatter and flatter, as it is dominated by the two-dimensional supporting surface and gravity. This may be appropriate for some ideas but not for others.

For this syllabus-building example I will start a little further on, with the additional aim of helping children to see how clay can be a building and constructional material. Therefore, the start is to encourage the experimental and inventive handling of clay as a constructional material. Each child is given a block of clay, say a four-inch cube, and asked to pull a piece of it. They then work with this to stretch and flatten it without using a base board. Rolling out, pulling and pinching, squeezing and pressing, are all ways of extending a small piece of clay to its ultimate, using fingers and palms as well as a base board. The resultant sheets of clay could be folded, bent, cut and made into tubes, all of which would begin to show the structural and three-dimensional potential of the medium.

The results of this first experiment should be looked at and discussed to see what ideas have arisen and how inventive the group has been and to share ideas and possibilities for further development. Teachers do not find this easy, as Viola realised in 1942.[1]

It is now necessary to show the group a simple method for joining clay together so that their experiments can develop further. The basic idea is simple and each one will find the best method to suit him. Clay, in a creamy state called slip, will act as an adhesive in joining two drier pieces of clay together. Either a small jar of slip, or a small ball of clay with a depression in which to add water with a brush until it becomes creamy, will suffice. Cautions about using water with clay should be given and it may be simplest to demonstrate the joining and wetting of clay. Clay is at its messiest when very wet or very dry and in these conditions should be avoided.

The range of small shapes already made could now be joined together with slip and other shapes be made to add to them. The lure to be inventive can now be very strong, though some of the more cautious or timid children will hold back, perhaps producing rather flat forms with pieces built up on them. After a short while the experiments can be shared and various points made about handling clay in this way — such as judging when the material has become too dry to work, feeling the section or thickness beyond which one cannot go for certain purposes, and successful ways of making joins. As clay dries on exposure to air, thinner sections of material will dry more rapidly than thicker ones and the rate of shrinkage between the two can cause cracking. Children will readily appreciate these points.

It is likely now that ideas will be flowing and a base could be flattened or rolled out on which to assemble the various things which are made. Some pieces will suggest fantastic ideas, others practical ones; children should be encouraged to attempt them but keep in mind the best practices for handling the material.

Further developments can occur when leather-hard tablets or sheets of clay are prepared. Clay in this state is firm but still flexible, so that it can be cut and joined, folded and impressed very easily, without either cracking or distorting. Clay in such a state is really nice to use and very different from when it is in its soft and malleable state.

To each of these developments should be added the children's looking, so that as soon as they are ready, they can interpret their buildings in the medium of clay. Apart from ideas arising from the direct handling of the clay, ideas may also be nourished from other sources, such as Peruvian or Etruscan models, modern ceramic artists and the children's own experiments in building with clay.

Narrative and literary ideas can be interpreted in clay and have a particularly magical quality because they are three-dimensional; that is they have space, depth, interior or exterior forms and so on. Thus the syllabus for clay can develop in various ways according to how children work with it and the kinds of sharing, looking and story-telling which goes on.

Repetition and building up of good practice and knowledge in handling clay will help children to use it with ease and confidence. The clay itself will suggest ideas for its use and ideas for work in clay will be suggested from experience in other arts and from the events and happenings of every day.

As three-dimensional medium clay can interpret all kinds of experiences and the way in which children can imaginatively inhabit the forms and constructions they create makes it a profoundly satisfying material for children to use. This relationship of children to clay is perceptively described in *Rosegarden and Labyrinth* by Seonaid Robertson.[2]

There are, obviously, many other ways of working with clay, using slips, oxides, moulds and so on and glazing and firing it. I believe that there are an enormous number of experiences children can enjoy with clay before getting involved in the more exacting

— Looking at and making drawing from the enviroment
— Exploration of clay as a material

discussion to focus attention on the way it behaves

exploration and more positive experiments in stretching clay to
some of its limits

joining clay pieces   small figures, plants, creatures

working with leather-hard clay   modelling and building up clay

tablets/sheets   building in
textured,   three dimensions,
impressed   adding to by slip
and built up   joining

looking at each other's work and the work of ceramic artists and
clay work from other cultures and periods

business of glazing. Painting and colouring clay can destroy its
natural qualities of colour and surface, and these should be ex-
ploited first, in my view, by using colour slips and oxides and not
paint.

I hope that these examples show a number of ways in which the
syllabus can grow from one's aims and response to the work and
ideas of the children one teaches. This kind of approach to building a syllabus is continuous and evolving, in that thinking through
each new session and reflecting on experience will change and
modify practice. This does not mean that aims are abandoned but
that they are modified, added to, and developed through the
experience of teaching and the observation of children learning.
Together with the children, the teacher can build up a range and
repertoire of ideas and approaches which can be used in innumer-
able ways to develop children's understanding and confidence in
art.

It is valuable for the teacher to note down the sequence and
development of the work he does with children as this will form
the basis of his syllabus-building ideas. This does not mean that
work will be repeated each time but that the teacher will increase

his understanding of how to make any experience more worthwhile and see more readily areas of progress and development in what children do.

To summarise, three examples have been given of ways to build up a series of experiences which develop and follow through the teacher's objectives but have the flexibility to accommodate children's responses and ideas as their work develops. Objectives are stated for each of these examples and possible lines of development described.

These desciptions are intended to show one possible method of building a syllabus and it is hoped that they encourage individual teachers to attempt their own approaches, both from their own thought and reading, and from the responses and ideas of the children they teach. Finding ways of recording what children do and the relevance and suitability of different ideas and developments arising from any activity is a necessary part of this process.

Notes

1. Wilhelm Viola, *Child Art* (University of London Press, 1942), p. 60.
2. Seonaid Robertson, *Rosegarden and Labyrinth* (Routledge and Kegan Paul, 1963), p. 82.

10 THE CHOICE OF MATERIALS

The careful and considered choice of materials, both in range and quality, makes all the difference to the work children do in art, craft and design. It is necessary for the teacher to categorise materials in order that they can be grouped and stored and that the range is as wide as financial and physical circumstances permit. For example, as well as drawing, painting and print making some kind of three-dimensional experience is, I believe, essential and every effort should be made to provide some form of material to make this possible. The suggestions made here are not intended to be comprehensive but it is hoped that they will show the kind of groundwork that needs to go into building up an appropriate range of materials.

There is clearly a need to supplement the comments and suggestions made in this chapter with other reading. To this end ideas are offered with examples of the kind of things to look for in supportive books. At the end of this chapter a number of books are suggested, more because of how they set about helping us to understand something of the background, possibilities and basic techniques of a craft rather than supplying a shopping basket of ready made things to do with children.

The choice of suitable materials for art and craft will be determined by various factors, such as the amount of money available, the space to store them and one's personal preference. The ease of use and facilities will also influence choice. It is not my intention to give a complete list of art and craft materials available on the market but to consider certain kinds of work along with the characteristics of groups of them. I believe that it is essential to keep the range simple and basic, adding to it other items as the teacher's experience and confidence to handle them with children increases. It is always easier to introduce different materials when the conditions and circumstances are right to do so, rather than clutter the classroom, the teacher and the work of the children, with lots of materials from which the children will receive only a transitory and shallow experience.

Areas of Work

In Chapter 8 I suggested possible areas of work necessary to fulfil
the aims of the curriculum, namely: (1) drawing, (2) painting, (3)
claywork, (4) print making, (5) fabric and thread. It seems sensible
to use this range as a starting point from which to consider the
choice of materals. Certain craft materials should be added to this
list, but these will depend on the locality of the school, the interest
of the children and the enthusiasm of the teacher. There are many
books available on different crafts, but careful choices should be
made of these. There are those books which relate to the traditions, developments, tools and practices of the craft, and those
which take a more didactic or prescriptive approach. Of the latter,
it is important to seek those which give basic information about the
techniques, use and possibilities of craft materials rather than
books which are full of gimmicks, visual tricks and easily made
results. The essence of the book should give the teacher sufficient
information to get started and insight into the craft to acquire confidence, and is not intended to supplant his own discoveries with
ready-made solutions. Examples are given at the end of this chapter.

1. Drawing

Mark making and drawing of various kinds are possibly the most
natural and accessible forms of visual expression and communication. The range and quality of drawing materials is considerable
and therefore requires careful study when making choices for use
in teaching art.   The stimulus and the intention behind the act of
drawing should be taken into account. Certain stimuli will suggest
corresponding choices of media, such as soft, fluffy objects with
chalk, or hard spikey ideas with pen and ink. Choices should be
made by the child though they can be intimated in various ways by
the teacher, always accepting that he should not be dogmatic
about correspondences he sees, and always open to the revelations
and experiments of children.

If money is to be saved, it can be done by careful selection from
different categories of materials and the judicious use of different
kinds of paper such as sugar, packing and brown papers. A limited
range of good quality drawing materials is better than a wide range
of inferior ones. The four categories set out below should help in
this respect.

Characteristics	Choice Range	Comments on Use and Extensions
Soft, smudgy	Charcoal } Chalk }	Use with sugar paper or toned, rough textured paper
	Pastel	Brown wrapping paper.
Blends and shades easily.	Thick leaded pencil Soft pencil (2B-6B)	Good in combination, light, dark, white, brown, black.
Needs fixing.	Charcoal pencil } Conte crayon }	
Waxy, greasy	Wax crayon Oil pastel Plastidecor	White cartridge paper. Firm paper required when building up surfaces and scratching into them.
Resists water.		
Builds up deposits.	Metallic wax crayons	Newsprint for making rubbings from natural and man-made surfaces or card blocks built up from wallpaper, fabric and card.
Can be scraped and scratched through.	Chinagraph Coloured pencils	
		White cartridge paper for wax resist — using paint or inks such as brusho.
Wet, runny	Inks Brusho	Used with brushes of different sizes.
Overlays of transparent colour.	Water based Indian/permanent Drawing inks	Pens, sticks, cards, quills. White cartridge paper to give maximum effect of transparency.
Mixes of colour.	Large felt tips Water colour sticks	White card to stop buckling.
Running one colour into another.	White ink	Black paper, pens, sticks, small brushes.
	Markers (spirit-based)	White paper or good cartridge paper.
	Water colour	Water colour papers. Good cartridge paper.
Hard and linear	Hard pencils HB/F	White cartridge paper, white card.
Makes lines, dots scribbles etc.	Ball points Fibre tips	Toned paper, manila, sugar paper in combination with other media.
Builds up surfaces, textures and tones.	Nibs and quills with various inks Mapping pens Draughtsman's pens Rolling ball pens	Cartridge paper

Every new art materials catalogue that is published seems to have a number of new drawing materials in it. It should be possible to place these in one of four categories as above. Some of these materials are similar to traditional ones but may be in a more manageable form such as charcoal pencils which unwrap rather than sharpen and square colour sticks of similar material to coloured pencil crayons.

Painting

The cheapest paint with the widest range — and therefore the best for general use in school — is powder colour, though it is not as fine nor as pure as other forms of pigment. Powder colour requires careful dispensing and should be kept and presented in a clean, uncontaminated condition. Mixing palettes, clean water and a rag or sponge to take up surplus water from the brush, help the child to manage the medium. It is sensible to restrict the range of colours stocked as this simplifies storage and dispensing and encourages children to be inventive in their mixing. The basic palette can consist of white and black, yellow, blue, and two reds, one tending towards crimson the other towards orange. Any additions to this basic palette might include yellow ochre, a green and a brown.

There are many other paints on the market, some specially prepared for particular uses, others extensions or refinements of existing pigments.

Liquid colour should be viewed with caution as it can inhibit real mixing and tends to dominate children when they use it, both in colour range and consistency. The teacher should aim at heightening sensitivity to such things as subtlety of colour, range of tone and texture, and relationships of areas of colour. These qualities arise as part of the process of preparing and mixing paint prior to applying it to the surface. Liquid colour seems ready for use and to require little attention to such things and therefore produces superficial or crude work.

Pots, tubes and tubs of poster colour are more refined than powder colour and therefore specialised in their use and more expensive. They are nice to use, giving good, opaque cover, and can be applied easily over each other, though they can dry with a rather dead surface.

Of the solid tablet forms of colour by far the best is water colour though it must be realised that there are different grades and qualities and that it is used differently from the other paints so far discussed. Water colour is ideal for delicate washes and overlays of colour. Qualities of fusion, transparency and atmosphere are a delight to achieve and generally work of a small scale is more suitable. It should be handled with small, soft, and the finest quality brushes that can be reasonably afforded. A wider range of colours is necessary in water colour to include more blues, browns, greens and yellows.

Water colour is best used on paper which has a slightly textured surface and special papers are available though generally too expensive for most school use. Cartridge paper of good quality and weight will do, say sixty to eighty pounds. The paper should be stretched before use, that is soaked in water and then stuck down around the edges with brown sticky paper. Stretched paper allows washes of colour to be applied without the paper buckling.

3. Clay

Clay is a natural material which has been dug from the ground and refined to take out extraneous matter. The chemical constituents of different clays vary considerably and affect such things as firing temperature and colour. The moisture content of clay is very important and it should, therefore, be kept in air-tight bags. The least hole or split will allow clay to dry out and eventually become unmanageable. Bags must be inspected on delivery. Clay is in its dirtiest state when too wet or too dry; clay in good condition is a real pleasure to handle and not messy.

There are three types of clay readily available to schools, namely grey, terracotta and raku. Each of these has particular properties in the manner in which it dries out and fires, and therefore each clay handles differently. All clays shrink on drying, some more than others. This shrinking causes cracking and distortion which can be overcome by the careful making of objects and careful, slow drying out. Raku clay shrinks more evenly though it is coarser to use. It is by handling materials that their limitations and possibilities are appreciated and children can become very versatile and inventive in the way they explore and experiment with materials like clay.

How clay is presented to children can make a considerable difference to the way in which they handle it. The material should always be in a good condition — neither too soft and tacky nor too hard and lumpy. It should not have bits or small lumps in it unless it has been specially 'grogged', as is the case with raku clays. Small lumps or spheres of clay will initiate a different start from pulling pieces from a large lump. How the fingers wrap round it, poke into it or tear it, can determine the way in which a piece of work develops and how the imagination is moved to work with the material. Clay that is soft and pliable but not tacky allows all kinds of forms to be made from it by pushing, squeezing, hollowing and adding.

Flat slabs of clay, small or large, allowed to dry to a leather-hard consistency, will show great rigidity and take impressions clearly, whether these are from tools, natural forms or scrap materials. Leather-hard clay also makes a marvellous constructional material, whether through building with slabs, or smaller pieces shaped for specific purposes. It is necessary to take care in joining leather-hard clay, as described in Chapter 9, so that it does not break apart on further drying out. All kinds of objects, buildings, constructions and environments can be built up from slabs and shapes of clay when it is in this condition, once children have mastered the simple technique involved.

4. Print Making

Put very simply, printing is concerned with the transfer of one surface to another. A painted mark blotted on to another piece of paper makes a print. Various ways of making more permanent surfaces for printing have been evolved and these constitute part of the craft of print making.

The simplest print surface is the momoprint which is a one-off method. A sheet of perspex or a plastic table top can be painted and marks scratched into the paint surface. A print can then be blotted from the surface which retains the marks made in it. Variations on this method can be made by introducing more than one colour and different means for altering the paint surface, such as combs, corrugated card and fabric.

The three major forms of more permanent and repeatable print making are (1) built-up blocks, (2) cut-away blocks and (3) stencils. Each of these provides endless opportunities and variations for creating printed surfaces on paper and fabric — for example by adding colours, modifying surfaces and overlaying prints.

The first essential, when working with children, is to get them to enjoy and respond to the particular qualities of printed surfaces and to help them to see how printed surfaces are different from painted ones.

The paint or ink used for making prints from blocks is, possibly, the most important ingredient to successful print making. Ordinary powder colour can be used if it is mixed with liquid soap or paste to help bind it and to stop the paint from drying out. However, it is not really suitable for obtaining good results and there are many water solvent printing inks available. Water-based and emulsion inks are very suitable for children to use and easy for them to handle. Older children can manage oil-bound printing ink which does not dry out so quickly and has a very even consistency. Oil-bound ink enables more varied, precise and finer print surfaces to be achieved than the other kinds, but it is more difficult to use. It is solvent with white spirit or turpentine.

The kinds of images that can be discovered and invented rely considerably on the nature of print making and it is important for children to look at and discuss prints as well as produce them, so that sensitivity to the process and its effects is heightened.

(1) *Built-up blocks.* Almost any material can be stuck down to form shallow, raised, patterned and textured surfaces capable of printing. The difference in height between layers should not be great: Card blocks are simplest, but string, fabric, wall papers, applied textures and natural materials and so on can be used as well. A PVA adhesive is suitable for sticking these down. There is plenty of scope for inventiveness here, but attention should be paid to the printing ink used and the method of application. The effect is for the raised parts to print as positive.

(2) *Cut-away blocks* include such things as potatoes, lino, polystyrene, soft wood and hardboard. The means for cutting or scoring can be lino tools, craft knives and gauges. Printing ink is applied to the surface and not the hollows and must, therefore, be of the right consistency. The effect is for the cut away parts to print negative.

A further development of this type of print surface is the use of copper, zinc or plastic sheet, where the surface is scored or eaten away by acid. The resultant etched and scored lines and textures are filled with ink and the surface wiped clean. A print is achieved by using damped paper and pressure to pull the ink from the surface marks. Of course, acid cannot be used by children, but the method does show something of a drypoint or etched quality of print with the fine and subtle qualities peculiar to this approach.

(3) *Stencils.* These are made by using a waxed or strong paper or thin manila card. The design is cut away with a craft knife or scissors and printing ink is dabbed or brushed through the stencil

on to the paper. An extension of this approach is the silk screen. Here, organdie, fine nylon or even nylon tights are stretched across a wooden frame. The cut away stencil is stuck to the surface of the screen and ink forced through the screen and the stencil by use of a squeegee. There are various ways of stopping out the screen and these form a separate study. There are special screen printing inks on the market, and it is advisable to use these for good results.

The possibilities for experimenting with different print surfaces and the variety of ways of making a print are endless. The important educational considerations are that the right attitude and approach should be encouraged in the children, who should be helped to work systematically and note their discoveries and discuss them. They should also be helped to see the potential of print making to transform simple, visual ideas into print images.

The quality of the ink, its dryness or stickiness, its colour and texture, the care with which the block is made up or the stencil cut, the manner, and pressure with which the print is taken, all require the attention and sensitivity of the child. The worst experience of print making that children can have is for them to turn out quantities of prints with no thought or understanding of what they have done.

5. Fabric and Thread

We all experience the sensations of fabrics and threads every day or our lives, through the clothes we wear, the furnishings in our homes and the materials around the places where we work. Tactile sensations from textures like softness, roughness and warmth, visual sensations like colour and pattern, and spatial sensations of draping, fitting round and covering are all part of the richness of fabrics. Strings, wools, cottons and twine are some of the threads with which we have almost daily contact.

Despite such supposed familiarity, children need to explore fabric and thread to find out how it behaves, its qualities and so on. The fact that relatively short fibres of various kinds are twisted together to make threads comes as a revelation to most children. It is also a surprise for them to discover the many different sources of fibres that go to make threads.

There are three basic forms of fabric, with many variations in composition, colour, pattern and texture, namely knitted, woven and processed. Examples of threads linked together by loops, knots and plaits can be found in such diverse things as netting, lace, knitting, crochet and macramé. Threads can be woven together in various ways on the principle of long threads (the warp) being interlaced by shorter ones (the weft). There are many methods for setting up threads to do this such as using a wooden frame or hanging threads with weights, and a complex loom is not necessary.

The third category of fabric is that which has been processed in some way, such as felt and plastic materials. These form an important group of diverse materials with distinct properties, but they are found in common use and are therefore very accessible to children.

There are many changes, additions and modifications which are made to fabric, such as gathering and pulling threads, cutting, joining and assembling, appliqué and embroidery and padding or quilting. Furthermore, fabric and thread can be altered by dyeing and printing, whether this is by excluding colour through tying, waxing or screening the threads and fabrics to achieve a change of colour or pattern.

All of these things indicate something of the potential richness and variety of fabric and threads. A basic stock of hessins, scrim, cottons, felts and tweeds can be built up to which can be added scrap fabrics. Children will usually bring bundles of fabric into school on request and these need very careful sorting so that just sufficient variety in colour, type and texture is added to the basic stock. Pieces of lace, ribbon, crochet, braid and nets, silks and velvets can be stored in a bag or box as special items to be introduced at appropriate times.

Similarly, a basic stock of strings, twines and threads can be collected to which can be added more special cottons, embroidery threads and different weights of wool.

As with any materials, pre-selection and careful presentation is vital if children are to be helped to make sensitive choices that will lead them to discriminate between different qualities and respond to the nature of fabric and thread.

Scrap and Waste Materials

All kinds of materials that can be salvaged from the packaging of commercial and industrial products seem to find their way into many classrooms. Such things as plastic cartons, packaging, cotton reels and insulation, polystyrene containers, cardboard and compressed paper, items from metal foil, off-cuts of wood, fabric and string and all shapes and sizes of boxes to mention but a few.

This assortment of waste products is put to a variety of uses, like print making, collage and simple construction. Many teachers feel that scrap and waste materials provide a cheap and useful source of work stuff which enables them to introduce certain kinds of work, such as collage and construction, and eke out the meagre rations of more traditional art materials. While not denying the validity of these points, it seems to me that nothing can supplant the right choice and quality of traditional art materials and that it is better to have a few good quality art materials than a wide range of poor ones supplemented by a quantity of waste and scrap products.

The crucial issue in collecting scrap and waste material is that the most careful discrimination and deliberate choice should be made. Choice should be determined by educational considerations rather than by novelty, variety and economics. I venture to suggest the following criteria for making selections from scrap and waste material.

(i) *The quality of the scrap and waste.* For example, the cleanliness, how it has been made, ease of handling in a classroom, and the form in which it is found should be considered. Large sheets of poor quality card, too thick for scissors to cut, absorbent and having stains and score marks on its surface, are totally unsuitable for most things, however large a quantity is offered.

(ii) *The means for cutting and joining should be compatible.* Plastic, polystyrene, cardboard, metal foil, polythene, and corrugated packing may all seem attractive but cannot be cut and joined with the same tools and adhesives. However superficially attractive the forms and patterns might be, considerable frustration can be experienced if the means and purposes for handling them are not thought through before having accumulated these materials.

(iii) *Careful selections should be made for known, anticipated or imagined purposes and not for their own sake.* The random collection of scrap and waste can be contagious and insidiously contaminate all the art work which a teacher undertakes with his class, as well as clutter whatever shelf and storage space he may have. It may have been found that certain cardboard boxes are ideal for print making or that imprinted wrappings are good for textures, surfaces and rubbings. Making such selections is a more sound way of adding to resources than indiscriminate hoarding.

(iv) *After careful selection, materials should be sorted, labelled and stored.* It is relatively easy for a teacher to collect scrap fabric from various sources. The essential task is to sort any collections into boxes using colour, texture, pattern and so on as categories for storage. The sorted materials can then be used as a 'palette' from which children can work and it will thus go a long way to help children to be selective and discriminating in how they use them.

(v) *Materials are devalued when they are abundant or collected in excessive quantities.* It is better to be over cautious when collecting scrap and waste so that it is looked at properly and not discarded or ignored because it is plentiful.

If children are going to make box constructions a considered choice of types, sizes and proportions, which can be stuck with the same adhesive, will go a long way to making their experience a positive one. It is important that children are given three dimensional experience but it should not become a series of frustrations which only the most persistent can overcome.

It is an essential part of the role of the teacher to select and present materials as well as he can. The choice and range of materials available will depend on many factors, not least the capacity of the teacher to organise them and keep them in good order. The best quality materials should always be aimed for according to individual circumstances. Enthusiasm and interest count for a lot, but the teacher is best advised to build up his knowledge and understanding of a few materials with the children rather than extend his and their experience too widely too soon. Children need time and space to explore and experiment through which they gradually enter an intuitive understanding of and develop a practical skill for a material at levels which are appropriate for them.

Display

Display is an important part of a teacher's work, particularly in the field of art education, for the visual environment can function in various ways to make a classroom or school a pleasant and inviting place where children want to be, to stimulate interest in visual things and a response to visual, tactile and spatial experience and to inform and educate people generally about art education.

Completed examples of children's work or work in progress can be used by the teacher to stimulate discussion about visual ideas, to make correspondences with other work, including that of artists and to generate new developments. This aspect of a teacher's work is discussed in Chapter 7.

Mounting children's art work enables it to be seen more clearly in its own right, separated from the visual confusion of materials in which it will have been produced. Mounts should be as simple in colour and style as possible; black, white and grey paper is sufficient to achieve good mounts for most work. A subtle, grey, pencil drawing on white paper can look really well mounted on a thin edge of grey paper placed on a broader white mount. Heavier drawings may require a thin black surround on white or grey paper.

Children's pictures should never be cut out with scissors in my view. This action destroys the subtlety of the edges of a drawing, painting or collage, where the mark of the pencil, fall of the brushstroke or edge of fabric is particularly important. Cutting out the work forces the cut shape on the visual attention rather than the shape taken by the piece of work.

When it comes to pinning up work, large headed thumbtacks should be avoided, as again they are visually disturbing. Pins, staples or Blutak enable the work to be fixed without the means being too obtrusive. Mounted work should always be set out on vertical and horizontal axes, with, as far as possible, the outside edges lined up rather than each piece being placed randomly. The purpose of these points is to make sure that the children's work is seen simply and clearly with a minimum of visual clutter, distortion or distraction.

Three-dimensional work can be displayed on boxes, bricks or blocks of wood cleaned down, painted or covered with paper or natural hessian. Drapes are often useful for covering unsightly areas, whether walls or old shelving, but should be arranged simply rather than in florid folds or gathered flounces.

All kinds of things can be brought into the classroom to interest children and stimulate in them visual, tactile and spatial responses. Displays of natural, living and man-made things can sensitise children in all kinds of ways, from helping them to appreciate the needs of living things to initiating their own personal looking and collecting. Children should be encouraged to touch and share displays and to contribute to them. All items should be introduced with care and well shown so that any precious or valuable items can be handled safely but naturally by children.

The way in which even the same things are displayed can bring out different qualities. For example, a collection of metal, rusted or tarnished items, can be placed on brown paper to bring out colour, or on different kinds of surfaces to bring out the textured qualities. A collection of dried seed heads can be set out with magnifying lenses to focus attention on their structure and mathematical arrangement or placed on a window-sill or on white paper to show up their silhouette. A collection of pebbles can stimulate interest in colour or roundness and three-dimensional form.

Other collections of objects might have a local or historical interest and be borrowed from a museum or local authority collection or loaned by parents. Displays of toys, pastimes, hobbies and so on can all generate interest and conversation and lead to visual as well as verbal responses.

Displays can have a number of different functions depending on where they are and the use to which they are put. Some will be mainly for visual interest and impact and might well be placed in public areas of the school; others will have a more specific educational reason and may include written material explaining the purpose and approach of a particular piece of work (see Chapter 7, p.113.)

However much time the teacher feels he is able to devote to mounting and display, it is clearly worth doing and worth doing well. Apart from any other consideration a room that is inviting and well organised is much nicer for the teacher and children to return to each day and spend time in.

Suggestions for Further Supportive Reading

Looking and Visual Concepts

Palmer, F. *Visual Awareness* (Batsford, 1972).

Rowland, K. *Visual Education and Beyond* (Ginn and Co., 1976).
'We must reveal the *process of Art* and not strain after superficial effects and the production of objects. If we can discover in

some of these processes a natural way of ordering the sensations received from the environment, as language is a natural way of ordering thoughts, children will produce not merely better objects but more creative responses to life in general. In short we must lead them to find a visual language.'

Tritten, G. *Colour and Form* (Batsford, 1971). Methods and ideas and presupposes: (1) 'a knowledge of the development of a young persons attitude to the visual arts from childhood to adolescence,' (2) 'a clear idea of the aims of art education within the framework of education as a whole.'

Printing and Pattern Work

Daniels, H. and Turner, S. *Simple Printmaking with Children* (Van Nostrand Reinhold, 1972). 'We hope that they show not only the reasons for using different print methods, but also various ways in which the problems of visual research can be approached. Children should be encouraged to think for themselves rather than master a number of visual skills.'

Green, P. *Creative Print Making* (Batsford, 1964). 'Printmaking here is not an end in itself but is used as a method through which the young person may develop his visual and tactile knowledge.'

Palmer, D. *Introducing Pattern* (Batsford, 1970).

Hartung, R. *Creative Textile Craft: Thread and Fabric, Creative Play Series* (Batsford, 1968). 'It is the essence of play that it should take place under certain limitations. The player, of his own accord discovers the manner of fashioning his play that is best suited to him.'

Maile, A. *Tie and Dye: a Present-day Craft* (Mills and Boon, 1967).

Russ, S. *Fabric Printing by Hand* (Studio Vista, 1964). 'For the beginner it would be best if he could approach each process with an open mind and, at first, let it teach him.'

Marsh, R. *Monoprints for the Artist* (Academy Editions London, 1973).

Other Materials

Seyd, M. *Designing with String* (Batsford London, 1967).

Berensohn, P. *Finding One's Way with Clay* (Pitman Publishing, 1974).

Farnworth, W. *Clay in the Primary School* (Batsford, 1973). '...

for much that is true about one's honest dealings with clay, is equally true about one's honest dealings with children. This easy affinity with a natural material lies at the heart of using clay. It is something to be nurtured and explored.'

Robertson, S. *Beginning at the Beginning with Clay* (SEA London, 1967).

Scott, G. *Approaches to Crayons, Chalks and Pastels* (Evans Bros.). 'At the beginning of each section describing the uses of a particular material you will be advised to experiment.'

Robertson, S. *Using Natural Materials* (Van Nostrand Reinhold, 1974). 'Seeing is one of the basic ways in which children get to know the world in which they are growing up.'

Laxton, M. *Using Constructional Materials* (Van Nostrand Reinhold, 1974). 'If children are to design and develop their own ideas, it must be appreciated that to insist on a measure of skill and ability to perform certain processes as a prerequisite to designing, is to misunderstand the nature of children's ideas and how they can be encouraged.'

Marcousé, Dr. R. *Using Objects* (Van Nostrand Reinhold, 1974). 'Personal response is inherent in visual awareness. It has to be recognised and carefully nurtured for it contains the germ of original, creative thought and expression.'

11 THE ASSESSMENT AND EVALUATION OF CHILDREN'S ART

It is my belief that we make assessments all the time that we are teaching. Sometimes the implicit or hidden criteria behind these assessments have to be brought out into the open, as, for example, when we are putting up exhibitions, writing reports or looking at children's work with other interested parties. What is the basis for our assessments and evaluations of children's art? If we never try to answer this question for ourselves much is lost to us and to our teaching. This chapter is an attempt to show one way the question might be answered and offers reasons for making the attempt.

Although examinations will not usually be encountered by children in the five-to-thirteen age range, it is nevertheless useful to make a distinction between examination, evaluation and assessment. Such a distinction will enable me to discuss the different ways in which chidren's art might be judged. The way in which a teacher works with children and views the results of their efforts will be considerably different depending on whether he is examining, evaluating or assessing. The structuring of available time, the choice of topics, the range of media and the expectations of certain kinds of results can all be affected differently according to whether the teacher is primarily examining, evaluating or assessing. Let me briefly distinguish between these three ways of judging childen's art in order to determine the most appropriate means for looking at and understanding the kind of art children produce between the ages of five and thirteen.[1]

An examination is conducted at or over a specific period of time in relation to clearly laid down areas of learning and categories of work. There is a definite curriculum with stated aims from which work arises and this is used to demarcate the area of work to be studied. It also generates the standards against which work is examined. Usually there is a range of experience and knowledge to be covered or with which the students are, at least, expected to be conversant. In art it has proved very difficult to set down or specify this range of knowledge because the acquisition of knowledge is only a small part of what might be expected to accrue from art teaching.

Certain abilities in handling materials, developing concepts and ideas as well as personal qualities of sensitivity, perception and imagination are all profoundly important and significant features of any outcomes of a course in art. These features are not to do with knowledge as such and are not so amenable to a simple form of examination. In fact, many things other than knowledge have to be considered by examiners which depend on their experience of art and their capacity to interpret the work presented to them. It is in the results achieved as pieces of art that many of the worthwhile outcomes of a course in art are inferred even though these cannot be examined as one might examine factual knowledge or learned technique. This is one reason why several pieces of work and such things as supporting studies, design sheets or sketch books, may be asked for, as well as examination pieces. Examination hardly seems the way to look at and judge children's art between the ages of five and thirteen.

Evaluation is rather different in that it may take place periodically and over different lengths of time. As with examination, evaluation takes place against a standard or set of values, however vaguely these might be expressed or inadequately described.

These standards or values are usually derived from a wider sphere than a particular situation or individual and therefore enable comparisons to be made between art work produced under different circumstances and by very different individuals. Of course it depends on the set of values and criteria that are used as to how effective any evaluation might be.

A teacher who moves from one school to another will take with him standards which he will have acquired; when advisers run in-service courses certain standards become apparent. Arising from these acquired standards, whether they are hidden or expressed, some form of evaluation of what is done is inevitable. In fact, the importing of standards is more likely to be by example than induction; by action rather than edict. This is because standards and particularly values tend to be embedded in people's attitudes and actions. For example, many teachers working in an education authority like the former West Riding of Yorkshire would have a good idea of what kind of art work was valued generally but this valuation was demonstrated by more than children's pictures and models. The art children produced, it was realised, sprung from a whole set of attitudes and ways of doing things which cared for children as individuals and respected what they felt and had to communicate. Aping the results of a teacher's work with children will not generate the same attitudes and ideas.

Nevertheless, it was possible to pick up certain traits in children's work which a teacher might recognise as being important and therefore worth striving for in their art teaching. For example, drawing and painting from the direct observation of natural forms — plants, animals and birds — became an important means to stimulate children's art in that Authority and the mark of it was detailed and careful representational work. Such work might be reproduced elsewhere by other teachers using such drawing as a standard against which to evaluate their art teaching.

Wider judgements of art activity can be extremely pervasive and do not reside only in teachers who are perceptive about art and sensitive to children. One must realise that all teachers use standards of some kind, often subconciously, and that evaluation is an integral part of teaching, whether such standards are derived from the teacher in the next classroom or a how-to-do-it book. The problem with values or standards which are acquired casually, so to speak, without the teacher thinking them through for him or herself, is that they can be ill-supported by educational thinking and lack of understanding of children. To put it bluntly, a teacher who has lifted a method or example from a book or magazine or colleague's classroom and uses this as a way of achieving results from children is still using a form of evaluation but in the worst possible manner. However a teacher works, it seems impossible for him not to evaluate what children do in some way, therefore, it is important that evaluation is recognised and thought through as part of the teacher's work. Guidelines and criteria for the range of activity and standards of achievement always exist whether set down, discussed informally or disguised as part of the hidden curriculum in art. It is from these that comparisons and evaluations are made. In my view, there are always values lurking somewhere, seeking recognition and being applied generally across a wide spectrum of ability and endeavour. It takes hard work, sincere effort and a degree of honesty to sort these values out so that they are appropriate to the educational level and tasks at which a teacher is working. The job of sorting out values can seem unending but it has its benefits and rewards.

First, the fact of having values gives the teacher the means to make and use observations of children learning and use these to evaluate the effectiveness of his teaching. If the teacher judges the value of his teaching on results alone, much of the purpose and benefits of his work will pass unnoticed. To feel secure with results only and not to relate to the child's experience of making art is to ignore a significant part of the child's learning. To wish to relate to the child's experience of making art is to ignore a significant part of the child's learning. To wish to relate to the child's experience is, of course, a significant idea in terms of teaching and evaluation.

Secondly, defining values gives an underlying sense of rightness, continuity and purposes to the teacher's work. It is easy for a teacher to feel at sea and anchorless in an ocean of conflicting ideas and attitudes if he has no values. Unless the teacher has found some underlying conviction he is always prey to any fancy gimmicks or new notions which come along, with the resultant feelings of impermanence and loss of purpose.

Thirdly, it is from sorting out values that real educational ideas arise, for it is having and developing ideas which continually revitalises teaching and renews the purpose with which a teacher works.

Evaluation, then, arises from a set of values, however these may be couched, and enables the teacher to have a general and comparative view of the work of an individual or a group. Both examination and evaluation say more about the results of a course of work than the particular educational value of any individual's experience although this is implied. The results assume the learning or lack of it as the case may be, whether this learning has developed skill, perception, inventiveness, sensitivity or some other capacity.

Evaluation obviously has its place in a teacher's work and I will return to this topic via the example aims later in this chapter in order to show how certain values, arising from one's aims, might be used in evaluation.

Assessment is different from examination and evaluation in that it considers the range of work and activities by an individual over a period of time, sometimes in relation to his previous work and sometimes in relation to the work of his particular group.

This long term viewing of an individual's art is profoundly important as certain qualities in his development will not be constant and therefore not evident in every piece of work. Qualities of perception, whether these are to do with visual qualities, like pattern or colour, or imaginative response, seen in the way ideas and images are handled, may not be apparent in one piece of work. Sensitivity to media, to handling their characteristics and qualities, and to objects and environments may not be evident in one piece of work either. This is not only because it is hard to turn on creativity, but much more to do with the kind of energy needed. Sensitive energies are necessary in the making of subtle judgements, visualising ideas and forming images from media.

Assessment, therefore, can help the teacher and pupil to become aware of particular strengths and interests. The teacher can help the pupil to build on these and to evolve some form of continuity and development in his or her work — for example, a sense of pattern developing towards or through print making; an interest in making and inventing extended through designing or sculpture. In this way assessment can become a positive tool to help the teacher plan work with an individual or group and reveal the shallowness and inadequacy of giving children something different to do each week or constantly changing the materials used.

Furthermore, the kinds of discussions that can arise when making individual or group assessments can increase everyone's understanding of visual and aesthetic matters and widen their range of perception. Any class of children can be divided into working groups which are arrived at through sharing and talking about the different strengths and interests within the class. (See Figure 11.1, p.190.)

As children's experience and knowledge of the world around them develops after the age of seven, they may adopt mannerisms, ways of doing things and clichés derived from their visual environment. The visual environment is very strong in our culture because of advertising, television and other forms of mass communication.

Outside the classroom a child might develop drawing skills by copying from these mass media and, although the drawings might be poor and inferior to those done at school, the child may place a particular value on the image. The same child might produce well observed plant drawings in class and not value them despite the fact that the teacher considers them beautiful. The teacher's task is not to oppose the subject matter which may interest or excite the child, but raise levels of understanding and sensitivity in the way media are handled and ideas are developed. Assessment enables a teacher to see how to do this because it encourages children to consider visual and aesthetic aspects of a piece of art independently from the subject content of their work. As has been suggested, soon after the age of seven children find themselves faced with the content/form tension and it is then that ideas about interpretation rather than copy need to be brought into focus and discussed. Assessment is one important means whereby this can happen.

Assessment makes it possible for the teacher to become aware

Figure 11.1: Playgrounds

These three drawings show the different ways in which childen understand spatial relationships. Each drawing used schema for the figures combined with observations or pattern making.

The first picture has a simple spatial idea with all the figures standing on the picture plane(edge) and little overlapping of shapes. The sky is at the top and the ground at the bottom.

The second picture shows a plan view of the playground space with figures and trees orientated to all points of the compass. The ring of figures is the only group seen in plan as if from above.

The third picture has shapes which overlap and most of the figures are correctly orientated apart from the one on the left and the above view of the three holding hands. The drawing shows a strong sense of the relationship between the different areas of the playground.

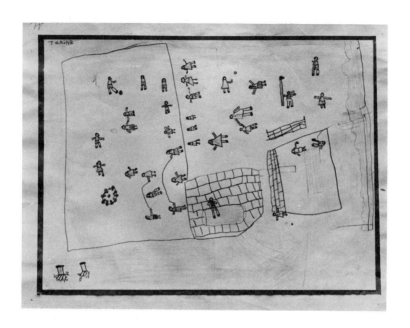

of individual strengths, inclinations and interests and from this knowledge build on successes and areas of confidence and consider potential routes for development. Assessment of a kind takes place practically all the time because it is the means whereby a teacher, often subconsciously, keeps the momentum of work going. When thinking about the kinds of things children might do next in art, the teacher will make decisions about the needs of his particular group which may be based on the way they work at present or how he envisages them working in the future. In some cases, and they may be more often than one suspects, the teacher may actually visualise the outcome of work before children start it and this can be the effect of the teacher's assessing what the children need on the basis of what they have already done.

Assessment, then, involves more than making partial judgements about a child's work at a particular time: rather it involves consideration of the work created by children over a period of time and takes account of the idiosyncracies, interests and forms of understanding which are peculiarly the individual's. Where no account is taken of these things a situation can be created in which the teacher's type of art is seen to be quite different from the child's art. It is almost as if the teacher's art had become a subject to be learned like any other and judged by a set of rules which only the teacher knows.

There is no doubt that as a teacher gains experience of talking with children about their art, the making of assessments becomes easier and more accurate and this has the effect of raising the general level of intelligence and understanding about art.

In the normal working situation of classroom of art studio it is seldom if ever necessary to make the kinds of judgements, or carry out the testing, demanded by examination or evaluation. However, it is important and valuable to make assessments or at least some estimation of the quality, direction, strengths and needs of a child's work in art. Assessment may include a careful study of the kind of marks made in a drawing, of the quality of shape or colour in a print, and discussion with a child or group as to how these have been handled. Assessment could involve the comparison of several pieces of work produced over a period of time. It could also include discussion of children's ideas, intentions and languages and the degree of understanding or insight they show in realising them.

An example of the kind of thing I have in mind may help. Having been asked to look at the art work of a group of boys and girls who were following a course at a comprehensive school, I looked at the folder of one of the boys. In this folder there was an assorted jumble of pieces — some completed, some unfinished or experimental, and scrap paper which should have been discarded. It was clear that he, like the others, had been following a series of topics, exercises and suggestions proposed by the teacher. Amongst the work in his folder were drawings, paintings, visual exercises and several poor prints from a lino block he had cut. When he was asked to pick out the pieces that gave him most satisfaction he chose a number which showed, in part, a feeling for and interest in pattern. This was spotted by one of the other boys in the group who entered the discussion about the various merits of his friend's work.

It was possible, now that the folder had been sorted out, to make certain assessments of this boy's work that he could share. It became evident that he had a feeling for pattern and would thrive on more opportunities to develop this aspect of his work. The observational drawings he had made from objects and his painting and prints all showed the same interest in pattern. This assessment of his work was obvious to his friends and became apparent to him, showing that further opportunities to develop the pattern quality of his work were a positive way forward. The linocut was the clearest example of how he had not been helped to do this. Line cutting lends itself readily to the exploitation and enjoyment of pattern, yet his prints were trite and clumsy, largely because he had not been helped to plan out or design from his own looking nor given the confidence and understanding to explore the medium in a personal way.

Thus, assessment is seen as an essential and valuable tool for the teacher, to enable him to support strengths, consider new directions, monitor progress and so on. Most teachers get to know the children they teach in such a way that they hold much of this knowledge in their heads, yet this has weaknesses which, in the end, can work against both teacher and child. It is all very well for the teacher to make intuitive and personal assessments, but these can still be read by children as biased assumptions. Assessment is at its most productive when it is shared with a child or children, for it can then focus understanding and observation so that everyone's intelligence about art is increased. Such considerations as the child's intention; what he or she had seen yet not beeen able to convey; his other responses to the medium, for example where accidents have been put to good use because the child was sensitive to the medium and recognised the possibilities in the way it behaved. These are some of the things that can become evident through shared assessment.

Assessment makes possible a level of sharing which widens and deepens understanding, whether such sharing of the work is within the group or through looking at the work of artists. The relationship betweeeen their forms of expression and those of recognised artists can help to give confidence and lead towards an insight about images. The boy in the above anecdote could have been helped to understand and appreciate the qualities and appearances of printed surfaces, the interaction between shapes and textures, the magic of colours overlapping and relating and so on.

To do the job of appraising children's work properly one should have more than a rough set of preferences from which to work. It should be possible for a teacher to arrive at criteria which act as points of reference or guide posts alongside which he can place a whole range of work. Some of these criteria will be easier to arrive at than others — for example those associated with the handling of media or particular craft skills. Other criteria will result from careful observation and discussion with children, such as those to do with perception, intention, understanding and sensitivity.

It is not easy to make an immediate start with assessment of this kind even though I have tried to show that, in my view, every teacher is assessing what children do for some of the time. There are, it seems to me, two fairly direct ways to get started, assuming that one sees the value of making more conscious assessments of children's art. One is to make collections of children's art work, or find some way of building collections, for example by using folders, notebooks or jotters. The second is to make notes on the kinds of observations and thoughts one finds oneself making when watching children at work or looking at the art they produce. Observations and simple notes are an appropriate way of recording some of the art work by young children, say of infant age. It can be practical to have older children themselves recording something of what they have done with the teacher making additional comments. Any notes or jottings can be ordered into some kind of simple record as will be indicated later.

Looking at and Recording Children's Art Work

The easiest way to start is probably by looking at the drawings by a group of children of the same age. Let us say that they have been looking at plants, specimens of which have been brought into the classroom. It will be assumed that the teacher has looked at the plants with the children and that they have talked about them together. This exchange will have brought into focus certain characteristics of the plants such as their patternn of growth, shape of leaf, texture and so on. The choice of medium is important and in this case is restricted by the teacher, to thick, well sharpened pencils, so that a range of tone (light and dark) and texture can be achieved.

The drawings which result from the children looking at plants will vary considerably and show a variety of different features. The age of the children will affect the kinds of drawing produced. Infants of five and six are likely to respond very directly and spontaneously to the nature and appearance of the plant. Part of its growth and particulars of its appearance may attract the child and be evident in the drawings in some exaggerated or schematic way. The child will use his existing vocabulary of marks to build on. Older children will tend to work out how the plant grows or fits together, show concern about correct proportion, notice details in relation to wholes and so on. They may even plan out or project the shape or pattern of the plant's growth before filling in the drawing.

Apart from considerations of the child's age, there will be differences in the handling of the medium, irrespective of the representational skills involved. There will be soft, searching, tentative grey lines in some drawings and heavy, solid, assertive, overworked dark lines in others. Some marks will show a facility and delicacy appropriate to some aspect of the object drawn, such as the soft hairs on the plant stem. These marks show a sensitivity to the object as well as to the medium.

There will be other drawings made in strong, direct lines, perhaps rhythmical or staccato, conveying a vigorous interpretation of the plant's growth or pattern. Or again, there may be drawings which show a facility for copying what is seen directly without close scrutiny, while others may not look as exact yet show some evidence of really close observation of detail. Of course there will be those drawings which show a lack of confidence or concentration. Each drawing will have something worth finding, if the teacher is observant and sufficiently patient to find it, whether it has been made by a six- or a twelve-year-old.

To start with, it may seem difficult to bring out specific qualities from every drawing and this is not necessary. From what has been said it is possible, by looking carefully at a few pieces of work, to sort out a number of elements from the children's experience of drawing which can be used as a means for looking at drawings and showing an understanding of them. For example, the following elements might be distinguished:

(1) Handling the medium — the range and variety of marks, the strength and rhythm, surface covering and texture.

(2) Observation — of shape, detail and relationship of parts. What is seen and said about the object, its textures, surfaces, patterns of growth, understanding of structure and so on.

(3) Interpretation — the particular way in which a drawing emerges from the activity of looking and mark making. The choices and selections made. Distortions, exaggerations, simplifications, the play of light and dark and so on.

It should never be assumed that distortion is just bad drawing or carelessness, for one is not assessing a mechanical, mindless activity when looking at children's art but a live, vibrant and continually changing response. Such a response is informed by knowledge but energised by emotion or feeling; it is made acceptable by explanation but given meaning through personal interpretation and ideas; it is understood more readily as description but has its effect in terms of appearance and image.

Therefore, the way in which a teacher shows awareness of the personal responses of children, as well as encouraging levels of appropriate skill and understanding, is most important. A child may develop a real feeling for an object, experience or situation which transcends direct description; it is then that the teacher has to see that this does not deny reality as he sees it but has a significance for the child.

If a teacher really looks at a child's work as well as the stimulus, it may well be possible for him/her to see the source of the child's response and understand better the art that has resulted. Reality, as a photographic likeness, is very limiting and the teacher should always be on his/her guard about using this criteria for assessment with no reference to the other forms of expression I have suggested.

It is possible to sort into various categories any collection of drawings from a group of children. These categories can be based on careful, direct observation of the drawings and may include the following categories: (i) those which use dark shading; (ii) those which show a sense of pattern in arrangement or detail; (iii) those which employ texture in scribbled, overlaid or clustered marks; (iv) those which reveal careful looking in parts of detail or delineating of shape.

Each of these aspects can be partly evident in some drawings and more so in others. To place drawings together which show similar aspects is to focus attention on these aspects and thereby increase the understanding children have of qualities of drawing. Such qualities as texture may have been brought out in the drawings or a number of children, irrespective of the correctness or accuracy of their representation. By focusing on textural qualities the teacher can show that there is more to drawing than copying. More important than this, the teacher can recognise that the meaning of an experience of plant for some children was embodied in its touch and it is this that they have brought out in the visual and aesthetic form of their drawing. (See Figure 11.2, p.198.)

This approach will widen the range of 'acceptable' drawing, extend the ideas and approaches used and help children to see that their own sense of what is important is valued. Leading from these kinds of considerations will be the possibility of talking about art as interpretation. Ideas about interpretation then make it possible to open up discussion about the content/form tension which enters children's experience of making art after the age of seven The way in which different media influence the appearance of a piece of art and change or modify an individual's ideas can be seen and compared when assessing several pieces of work.

Another rather similar approach is to collect all the art work of one child and look at it, with him or her, as a whole. This will reveal certain inclinations, interests, aptitudes, strengths and weaknesses and thereby enable the teacher's assessment to be shared positively with the child. New ideas, approaches and possibilities will then arise from what the child has already accomplished and can be discussed in terms of the content/form tension which has to find some resolution through interpretation rather than description. The increase in the child's intelligence about art

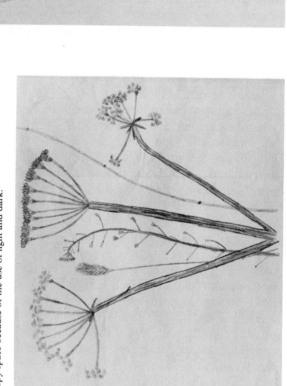

Figure 11.2: Plant Drawings

Each of these drawings shows a different emphasis in the way the medium is used and in the nature of the response to the object. The first drawing has a pattern quality. Note the seed heads and flowers and the arrangement of stalks. The second drawing shows an awareness of light and dark, the play of shadow across the stems and in the way one part of the plant crosses another. The seed heads seem to occupy space because of the use of light and dark.

through his/her own work will be as much to do with his/her understanding of interpretation as the handling of media and careful observation.

Folders or drawing books could be made available in which an individual's drawings are accumulated, including those made outside school, and all of these can give a good indication of the interests and sources of skill to which a child is drawn. Such a record could be particularly useful after the age of eight — say in junior and middle school, where children are much more influenced by second-hand imagery. Perhaps a few children at a time could be encouraged to put up small one-man shows of their work for others to enjoy. The object of this for the teacher is to be able to assess areas of interest, levels of skill, qualities of observation and so forth.

The teacher could devise a simple record card to go with some of the work produced as the keeping of a record can be an integral part of making assessments. However such a record is set out and whatever information or comments it contains, it can always be changed, refined, simplified or developed until it becomes appropriate to the groups being taught and properly serves the teacher. It is a good idea to attempt to sort out a record relevant to one's needs and simple enough to be completed easily. A system of cards, or a record book, could be used, initially to carry information and notes which arise directly from the teacher's exchange with the child about specific pieces of work. Recording every piece of work need not be undertaken but eventually one might extend recording, if it proves its worth.

This might be a possible record card for art:

1. Name:	2. Date:	3. Class:
4. Description and subject:	5. Medium:	6. Comments on Child's Interpretation
7. Quality of Observation or Invention	8. Handling of Medium. Skill and Understanding	

Note: The child could complete 1–5 and the teacher 6–8.

For the kinds of things on which the teacher could comment refer to Chapters 7 and 9.

As the teacher reviews the comments he makes, some will seem inadequate, others too complicated, some irrelevant and others missed out. However, this should not daunt him from pursuing some kind of record-keeping. It will be necessary to arrive at more precise descriptions of the child's activity, possibly by using a scale — say 1 to 5 — as well as descriptions or words. Such a scale could be devised from descriptions such as: very observant 1; quite observant 2; observant with help 3; sometimes responds with help 4; needs considerable help in looking 5.

The same arrangement might be used where some comparative scale enables changes to be recorded, but such assessments are obviously related to the kind of observation with which the child is involved. Direct observation is one aspect; that related to memory and arising from the imagination is another.

Thus, observation might become a more exact notion as the teacher thinks about it and watches children working. The way in which infants add to or extend their own schematic drawings might be evidence of heightened powers of observation in young children. Evidence of this heightening of observation could include such additions to their figure drawing as patterns, hair, texture, eyelashes and so on. The drawings of older children might show evidence of how things work, fit together or behave, as well as specific details of observed objects.

Then there is the other aspect of observation which is important, that of looking at one's own art and that of others. Here the child's perceptions can become very acute, both of the particular ways in which visual ideas have been achieved and the effects they create. Instinctively, a young child might distort the shape or colour of an object. Infants will do this spontaneously using their vocabulary of marks and schemata to set down their particular way of seeing and responding to something. Older children may change or distort an image because of an over concentration on a part of it or through an exaggerated response to its qualities or characteristics. Children of junior school age do need help in how they look at their work and develop a critical awareness in sharing work with others.

Over a period of time it will be possible for the teacher to build on his practice of looking at and discussing children's art precisely because the assessments he makes have become more objective and more clearly specified. That is, the teacher has become more aware of positive changes in approach, attitude and confidence, and found ways to describe these changes more exactly. Perhaps it would be useful to re-state the possible advantages of making some kind of assessment with or without the associated record system.

First, there are the reasons to do with helping children to develop a confidence and understanding about the art they produce related to their strengths and aptitudes.

Secondly, there are the reasons which arise from the need to encourage some kind of continuity and development in the teaching and learning which goes on.

Thirdly, there are the reasons which relate to the knowledge and confidence of the teacher concerning children's art, the appropriateness of his teaching, and the quality of his observation and understanding.

Assessment and Evaluation Based on Aims

In a similar way to that for developing the curriculum, I will suggest one possible approach to assessment and evaluation arising from initial aims.

Example aims:
To raise levels of sensitivity in children to the characteristics and qualities of art materials, the kinds of marks and forms they make and the images they can create.
To heighten children's visual, spatial and tactile awareness to the world around them.

If these example aims state, very broadly, what a teacher hopes to achieve, how does he know if the art children do and the outcomes from it are successful? It is so broadly stated that, to make any headway, certain criteria would have to be stated, and these would need to be seen as principles, characteristics and measures by which the teachers could determine any progress towards fulfilling, even partially, his aims. The point of having aims of some sort is to enable planning, direction and some kind of development to take place which embraces all the children and not just those who can make passable drawings.

From the stated aims it is possible to set down criteria, whether in single words or simple sentences, which can act as principles or guides for appraising children's work. Criteria, once arrived at, will help the teacher to look at and develop children's art and, as they become more familiar to him, he will use them with greater confidence and less effort. Criteria should not form rigid expectations but be as much like sensors, enabling the teacher to feel his way and maintain a sense of balance and direction in his teaching. Although they may hold the work on course they should not constrain or imprison it in pre-determined ends.

Let us, therefore, look at the example aims and the kind of criteria which associate with them, together with the kind of activity children might be pursuing.

Example Aim	*Activity of Children* which has been stimulated, extended or developed by teaching.
(1) To raise levels of sensitivity to the characteristics and qualities of art materials.	
Children handle materials with care, interest and focused attention	touching, mixing, spreading and applying media. Looking at and reflecting on work; responding to marks made: asking questions, making observations, answering questions. Stillness as well as activity; enjoyment and concentration.
Children explore and experiment with materials and show increased understanding of them.	ordering and shaping, repeating and inventing with materials, showing curiosity and confidence in handling materials and ways of applying them.
Children notice the effects that different materials produce and can talk about them	sharing and talking about appearances and effects of media. Repeating, developing and applying them. Using discoveries with confidence and increased fluency.

(2) To raise levels of awarenes to the marks and forms art and craft materials make.

Criteria:

Children develop perceptions about what materials can do.

controlling and organising materials; inventing solutions getting ideas and talking about them.

Children invent with and organise materials in different ways.

trying things out. Accepting and using chance effects developing ideas and images through handling materials and working out solutions to visual, spatial and constructional problems by experiment and innovation.

Children show more skill and control of media.

applying discoveries, working expressively as well as methodically. Making choices selecting appropriate tools. Discriminating between different media for different expressive needs, applying techniques, using methods they've been shown.

Children get ideas from handling materials and respond to the qualities of media.

talking about experiences with materials and media. Repeating, adapting and using in other ways ideas they have discovered, borrowed or been shown. Capacity to work out ideas and approaches for themselves.

(3) To heighten visual, spatial and tactile awareness to the world around them.

Criteria:

Children draw attention to things around them and notice displays in the

questioning, observing, analysing and making comments. Sharing classroom and things that have been brought in.

experiences and objects by touching and handling, recording what has been noticed in some aspect of their art, in detail, colour, shape or in their verbal descriptions.

Children are able to talk about and share objects, pictures and experiences of the world around them

pointing out and drawing attention to something showing that aspects of design, appearance or content of objects, environments and works of art and craft have been seen by talking, drawing, asking questions or making observations.

The activities of children can be described by each teacher from their own observations and any such observations that are made will be sharpened by the act of writing them down. Also, we should not be afraid of re-defining our aims and criteria as our experience develops and our perceptions of children making art change.

Furthermore, as well as guiding a teacher's assessment of a child's development in art, these criteria can be applied to a wider set of work than that arising from one group or individual. The problems of criteria being used in a wider context arises when certain of the criteria presuppose having a deeper knowledge of the children than is possible from looking at their art work alone, for example from having spoken to the children and perhaps having watched them at work. Hence, a general experience of having looked at children's art helps when applying given criteria to other groups of children than those whom you know and teach directly.

Certain kinds of action and ways of thinking and understanding leave their traces in the art work children produce. For example, a well observed drawing shows evidence of careful or detailed looking. Sensitivity to colour or shape and the way colour is mixed and employed is evident in the work that is produced. Evidence of the way in which an older child has analysed an object and developed ideas from this analysis for some kind of print or design will be apparent in his work.

Evaluation, based on one's aims, should seek to observe changes of various kinds which one hoped to bring about through the various strategies of teaching. It is these changes which need to be specified in some way so that they guide the teacher's looking. His understanding of children and his knowledge of art will also be important factors in any evaluation which is made.

Areas of Change

Let us say that four areas of change can be identified as follows:

1. Response. Children's responses will change as they mature and certainly be very different after seven years old, as has been described in Chapters two and five. Other changes related to these, but significantly arising from teaching, can become apparent in practical matters. For example, a willingness to observe closely, even examine and investigate; a capacity to explore, through a medium, the qualities, structure and appearances of something; confidence to question, discuss and experiment; an ability to plan and design; or the understanding to work directly yet carefully with a medium.

Another set of changes will be concerned with intention and meaning, especially as children approach and enter puberty. The kinds of subject matter, interests, and content of what is done, will change. Different kinds of things, ideas and visions will surface, which change what is valued by the child and the convictions with which he/she works.

2. Handling the Material. Continual experience in handling a material develops a fluency, confidence and skill with it that becomes apparent. Children will invent with and adapt a medium to their own creative ends which will show clearly their understanding of its properties and characteristics. For example, children who are used to handling clay will have a sure grasp of its drying properties and intuitively sense when it is right to handle in some ways and not in others; when it will mould easily or when it is right for making slabs. Infants, who have been given the trust and confidence to mix their own powder colour, will show an ability to handle the properties of the medium and enjoy the range of its qualities. Other children can become intrigued with techniques and processes, adapting and extending them in imaginative ways. Mastery of a material can give satisfaction but seldom at the expense of the ideas it serves. Both delicate and vigorous handling can show understanding where a material may be guided and coaxed or allowed to flow and expand. In both cases the way in which it communicates will have a clearity, certainty and perhaps spontaneity about it.

3. The Capacity to Communicate. The capacity to communicate through a material will depend on a number of factors apart from the skill in handling it. Young children will relate through a drawing, painting or model to the things they have noticed. Their perceptions of shape, texture or colour will change as their observation develops. The art of making a visual statement will, of itself, sharpen such observation and heighten the capacity to communicate. The schema of young children will change in what is added to them, in the variety of marks used and in complexity.

Older children will communicate, through their art, ideas and ways of understanding how things work and fit together, spatial and constructional notions which arise as a result of their investigations and discoveries. The way in which children talk about their work and that of others will also show how their capacity and need to communicate develops.

Although the skill to communicate ideas, feelings and understanding may sometimes be weak, it does not mean that the need is not there. Other experiences, apart from the skilled handling of materials, are necessary to enable the capacity to communicate to become manifest. The teacher should notice how the pupil uses opportunities to explore media and experiment with techniques; to discuss the visual and aesthetic qualities discovered and how they might be employed to interpret ideas visually. All these things can identify important changes in the aesthetic development of children.

4. The Development of Ideas and Interpretation. Describing or representing what is seen or experienced is not sufficient to communicate how one has been affected by it. The art of the pre-seven year old shows us as much about their direct response as it does of their understanding. Their pictures and models are as much schematic interpretations of their experience as descriptions of it. This is because their experience of the world is egocentric and depicts the essence of the thing portrayed as it affected them. Older children of junior and middle school age are able to build concepts from experience and use their ideas to relate these to their understanding. Therefore, the development of ideas and ways of understanding and making connections between things is very important and should be evident in their art and how it changes. Juxtapositions, relationships, experiments and explanations, which can be seen in their art, and arise in their talking about it, are ways of evaluating changes.

The need to interpret rather than copy will also become apparent from what children do at home if not at school. They can be shown how visual ideas are borrowed from various sources for specific reasons. They can then be encouraged to attempt to use visual ideas that excite them from borrowed sources in personal and imaginative ways. When such borrowing goes on the quality of drawing and handling media is often inferior but the ideas and connections may be reaching out to new horizons.

The Evaluation Sheet

If one now places these four categories of change (and there may be others more appropriate to different teachers with different aims) on an evaluation sheet, it is possible to look at and compare the work of different individuals or groups. This evaluation sheet should be used as a way of looking and not as a hard and fixed control of what children do. Therefore, it can enable a teacher to keep in mind a balance of qualities, each of which can develop through art education.

Figure 11.3 shows how an evaluation sheet might be set out and filled in. The 1-5 scale would have to be worked out by each teacher to suit his needs and would be modified as experience of looking at children's art developed. The four areas of change would show the teacher the strengths and weakness of each child both enabling him to appreciate what a child can do and where a child might best be helped.

A possible scale of evaluation of change in a child's art might be as follows:

1. Confident, competent and sensitive.
2. Confident and skilful.

3. Committed and interested.
4. Committed but needs some support.
5. Needs support and basic experience.

This scale should arise from the teacher's observations of children making art and be used to guide his work with them.

The following comments, based on the evaluation sheet in Figure 11.3, give a summary of each child's work over a period of time.

Arblaster A.	Ideas rather limited. Enjoys handling media but rather repetitive hence limits capacity to communicate.
Arbuthnot C.	Getting some good ideas and communicating well both in what she says and in the handling of the medium — considerable development.
Catchpole P.	This last piece shows how he had really got a good idea and knew how to interpret it through the medium. Swept along by his discoveries with the medium his response to the stimulus was less.
Day Q.	Remarkable change in how he responded to the stimulus, leading to a new and confident handling of the medium. Talked well about it though still not many ideas of own.
Ferris P.	Caught on how to interpret atmosphere with watercolour though got into a mess with it. Response to stimulus less effective.
Green T.	Still doing his thing but communicates well his interest and has nice ideas. Handling media still needs attention and may give breakthrough to new response.
Houghton R.	Beautiful interpretation of stimulus and response v. good but needs a lot of help with handling media. Not very communicative.

This evaluation sheet has been developed from the thinking about aims and directions for the work children do at different ages coupled with the observation of how they work and the kinds of things they produce. The evaluation sheet may not suit everyone but it is hoped that the thinking behind it will show the way to approach the task of evaluation and the positive results that can

Figure 11.3: Sample Evaluation Sheet

EVALUATION SHEET 5|6|93 Form 1 Ak. name of child	description of work	media	change in response	handling of material	capacity to communicate	development of ideas & interpretation	comment
Arblaster A.	Object Painting	Powder Colour	3	2	3	5	Must talk ideas and share objects
Arbuthnot C.	"	"	2	1	2	2	find her direction
Catchpole P.	"	"	2	1	1	1	Change to more dramatic stimulus.
Day Q.	Drawing Object	Charcoal Chalk	1	1	2	5	Talk about images and look at pictures.
Ferris P.	Object Painting	watercolour	3	4	1	2	Experiments with media (and Houghton).
Green T.	"	Powder Colour.	5	3	2	1	Wrong stimulus. Try getting him to bring something in.
Houghton R.	Drawing. Plant	Ink + chalks.	2	5	4	1	More experiments to give confidence with this new media.

come from it. It is not easy to make written statements about our teaching, nevertheless I believe the effort is necessary and that it has important outcomes for teaching.

To summarise, after discussing the different functions of examination, evaluation and assessment, the way in which I believe teachers use assessment continually, when they are teaching, is discussed. Assessment is thought of as a positive and necessary part of every teacher's work and examples are given of how this might be so and the further kinds of assessment which might be made.

A number of elements of children's drawing are distinguished from which drawings can be placed into categories. Criteria for assessment and evaluation are then suggested, based on example aims, which lead to a consideration of observable changes in the pattern and development of children's work.

Consideration is given to the kind of evaluation sheet that might be evolved in order to look at and possibly compare the work of different groups of children.

Note

1. *The Arts in School* (Gulbenkian Foundation, 1983), pp. 130-2.

12 CONCLUSIONS

This book has been written in order to share a number of ideas and observations about children and art education with fellow teachers, parents and all those interested in the development and education of young people. Since 1969, when I worked for four years for a Schools Council Project, I have given considerable thought to these matters and tried to write and talk about them. Throughout this time I have believed, with increasing conviction, that each person has to find ways to think through for themselves what and how they teach. Certain approaches and beliefs find favour or come into fashion from time to time and act as a stimulus to ones own thinking or, if allowed to, dominate it. Whatever we do as a teacher of children there is no excuse for not thinking about why we do it. I say this for two reasons, firstly, because we owe it to ourselves to continue to believe that each of us has something significant and worthwhile to give as a teacher and that this should never be allowed to go stale, dry up or die.

Secondly, because we owe it to children to always wonder, question, think about and respect the quality of young lives that only pass once through our care and are all too soon adult.

In reading biographies or listening to others reminisce, the frustrations, disappointments, discouragement and neglect that have, in various ways, turned them away from expressing themselves creatively, make sad listening.

There is a very deep wish to find ourselves, to be able to make some personal and telling mark on the seemingly indifferent uncaring and often hostile world of which we are a part. All too often the experiences which inhibit and frustrate any action of adults to remedy this situation for themselves are traced back to some bad childhood experience.

Those things which we do as teachers, which affect how children feel rather than what they know, have long lasting effects. The sense of failure and general lack of confidence, which we learn to disguise or cover up as we take our place in the adult world, have a nasty way of catching up with us as the patterns of work and home settle into a routine and many of our worldly ambitions are not realised or grow stale.

It is, therefore, of profound significance that one aspect of a child's personal experience, recorded in the things he/she creates, should be supported positively and given every chance to help him/her. How is any teacher going to find the time and incentive to go on thinking through what they do?

It is hoped that this book is one of several that will offer positive support to teachers in this task. It is not meant to be a compendium of solutions or provide the answers to all problems, it is truly meant as a means of sharing and a way of stimulating personal reflection and activity.

There are other means of achieving some measure of support to go on thinking, questioning and developing ideas and I describe some of these now.

In any school, where two teachers are able to discuss and question what they do, a feeling of mutual support arises which can sustain positive criticism and possibilities of change. Such discussion and questioning can start from anywhere, whether from the arrangement of their rooms and storage of materials; ideas on display or the kinds of things children do when producing art.

It could be that two teachers find ways to collaborate, complementing each others strength and, in so doing, giving each other confidence to try out new approaches and share their observations and understanding of children and discuss the results of their teaching. Such sharing can enable a teacher to develop particular strengths and enthusiasm, say, for example, for a craft. The knowledge and confidence which this produces can give a teacher a new lease of life but it also requires the continued discussion with and support of a sympathetic colleague. In this way the teacher will have the confidence to try new approaches but not deny the ideas, interests and ways of doing things that are the children's.

Discussion of such basic issues as the balance between direct teaching and unobstrusive support is best handled in a group where confidence has already been established to share ideas and practice. There are many similar issues which this book raises, such as progress and assessment in children's art, which require constant review and which is best guided by the sharing of ideas and practice.

The guidance of ideas and possibility of sharing in an atmosphere that is not threatening can often be found on in-service courses. It is sensible to choose such courses with care, knowing who is running them and the quality of their work. In this way it is possible to meet up with other teachers with whom you have had previous course experience and, therefore, some continuity of discussion and the further extension of ideas becomes more possible. A series of sessions or long courses are always valuable from the point of view of who you meet and the conversations you have in between organised sessions.

In many Education Authorities it has been found that an Art Education group is most valuable and rewarding if there are few in-service opportunities provided. The groups that I know of this kind include teachers from all levels of education, from nurseries to colleges. It requires a group to get together and set out a programme of talks, visits, meetings, exhibitions and so on. The choice of pleasant surroundings, with objects, flowers and displays of work helps to create the right relaxed environment in which people feel able to commit themselves to shared discussion. The provision of refreshments of some kind can also help considerably. Any local authority should be prepared to help in finding a venue and some cash to get the group off the ground. Local advisers and inspectors are always helpful or some member of the administration could be approached via the Education Officer. I have spoken at many such gatherings and have been impressed by the quality of thinking, discussion and organisation.

Lastly, but by no means least, it is most important that those who feel concerned and excited about children making art should find ways of sharing their understanding and enthusiasm with headteachers, and teachers working in other curriculum areas. It is not easy to find the right words to talk about children's art and craft experience and what this means educationally, nevertheless, I have found few headteachers who are not themselves concerned about this aspect of children's education and want to see the Art Education in their schools strong and vibrant. Every time we attempt to discuss and explain our understanding of children's art it makes it easier to do so in the future. Every time we neglect to do so or duck the issue, it makes it more difficult for our own thinking to develop.

Therefore, the final plea of this book is that each one of us should never cease to wonder at and think about the creative and imaginative potential that is manifest in children and evident in their art. It is profoundly important for the development of the human mind and spirit that we continue to seek ways to interpret our experience in the images and forms of art and that we always value this experience in the education of children.

INDEX

In compiling this index my concern has been to highlight certain words which, when referred to in the text, bring the reader near to the main arguments and issues which are considered in the book.